DEV
DURABLE MIND
A guide to cultivating adaptability and strength
BY DANTE POOLE

Developing A Durable Mind

A Guide to Cultivating Adaptability and Strength

By:

Dante Poole

E-Book: 978-1-300-55196-6

Paperback: 978-1-300-55194-2

Hardcover: 978-1-300-55192-8

Dedication

To *TEAM POOLE*, you are an incredible source of strength and inspiration. Your love, resilience, and shared vision to Educate, Equip, Empower, and Engage remind me daily that true durability is built in community.

PREFACE

In a world that constantly challenges our ability to adapt, learn, and grow, the concept of a durable mind has never been more essential. Developing A Durable Mind is a powerful and transformative journey into understanding the power of our own thoughts, examining the reasons behind our mental frameworks, and ultimately reshaping them for resilience and success. Through a unique blend of reflective exercises, relevant scenarios, and the wisdom of children's stories, this book invites readers to explore and challenge their own cognitive habits in ways that are both engaging and deeply personal.

What makes this book stand out is its innovative approach to personal development. The use of children’s stories as a medium to convey complex ideas is nothing short of brilliant. These narratives, often perceived as simple, serve as profound lessons on mindset, perseverance, and adaptability. They allow readers to reconnect with fundamental truths that are often overlooked in adulthood. The conceptual frameworks and self-reflection sections further solidify these concepts, encouraging active participation rather than passive consumption.

At its core, this book is about breaking free from a fixed mindset—a way of thinking that confines us to perceived limitations and keeps us from realizing our full potential. It provides a roadmap to cultivating a growth mindset, one that fosters continuous learning, resilience in the face of challenges, and a willingness to embrace change. The strategies outlined within these pages are not just theoretical; they are actionable steps that can be implemented in daily life to create lasting transformation.

What truly makes this book an amazing read is its ability to provoke thought and self-examination. It does not merely offer solutions but asks the reader to engage in meaningful introspection. Why do we think the way we do? What past experiences have shaped our beliefs about our abilities? How can we reframe our thinking to become more adaptable and open to new possibilities? These are the questions that form the foundation of this work, urging us to take an honest look at our mental patterns and to take ownership of our growth.

Resilience is not an inherent trait but a skill that can be developed. This book serves as a coach, guiding readers through the process of strengthening their mental fortitude. It equips us with the tools necessary to break free from limiting beliefs, navigate obstacles with confidence, and ultimately, build a mindset that is both durable and dynamic.

Whether you are seeking personal growth, looking to inspire change in others, or simply interested in understanding the mechanics of mindset, this book is a valuable companion on that journey. Prepare to be challenged, inspired, and empowered as you embark on this transformative experience. This is not just a book; it is a blueprint for mental resilience and a testament to the incredible capacity of the human mind to evolve. Let the journey begin.

Dottie Rains-Dowdell, DHSc

ACKNOWLEDGEMENTS

Books are never written in isolation. They are always the product of the input of the people in the author's life, the context of their life and wisdom gleaned from experience. This book is not different and would not have been possible without the support, encouragement, and wisdom of so many people.

To the authors of the children's books referenced throughout this work, thank you for crafting stories that hold profound wisdom in their simplicity. Your words have shaped minds, sparked imaginations, and taught invaluable lessons, not just to children, but to all of us who are willing to listen.

To my friends, colleagues, mentors, and accountability partners—your encouragement, insights, and belief in this project have helped bring it to life. Your presence on my journey has been a constant reminder that we are not meant to develop durability alone.

To the watchers and listeners of my podcast and those who engage with me on social media—thank you for being part of this ongoing conversation. Your reflections, questions, and shared experiences have deepened this work and reinforced the importance of building a durable mind together.

And to every reader who picks up this book, thank you. May these pages serve as a guide and a reminder that developing a durable mind is not just about enduring, but about growing, adapting, and thriving.

TABLE OF CONTENTS

Introduction

It was late one afternoon as I sat at my desk, holding my head in my hands, because my head was pounding. As a school principal, I was giving everything to the work of educating other people's children, supporting a hard-working staff, and pouring into a beloved school community. The problem was that I was doing all of this at the expense of my own health and well-being. How did I get here? When did this become my reality? I realized I hadn't arrived at this point suddenly. This was the result of a slow, deliberate drift into a work ethic that was valuable to others but was costing me my life.

Was this truly the expectation of a principal? Arriving before everyone and leaving after everyone? Working at my desk, in my car, at my kitchen table, and sometimes even in bed while my wife sat next to me watching a movie or reading? Somewhere along the way, my definition of success had morphed into "doing whatever it takes"—translation: giving it all and leaving nothing for those I loved most. I knew something needed to change, and it began with a deep dive into my own thinking. It wasn't that my actions were wrong; it was my mindset that had gone astray. I had surrendered my commitment to a decision I made years earlier—not giving my best to everyone else and leaving the scraps for my family. I had allowed the demands of my work and my desire for success to cause me to break that promise to myself.

The Stories We Tell Ourselves

We all live within the stories we tell ourselves, narratives shaped by experience, expectations, and the quiet dreams that whisper in the background of our lives. Sometimes, those dreams give us direction, fueling us with purpose and possibility. Other times, they become distorted by pressure and perfectionism, turning into stories of exhaustion, self-doubt, and fear of failure.

I had allowed my own story to become one of depletion, written by the belief that success required sacrifice at all costs. But as I sat there that day, overwhelmed and weary, I knew I needed a new story—one where durability was not about enduring exhaustion but about developing the mental strength to navigate life's challenges with wisdom, balance, and intention.

That's when I began to explore what it truly meant to develop a durable mind—one that could withstand pressure, adapt to challenges, and thrive in the face of adversity. Through my journey, I identified five key attributes that shape this kind of mental durability, summarized using the acronym **D.R.E.A.M.**:

- **D**etermination – The ability to remain committed despite challenges and setbacks.
- **R**esilience – The strength to recover, rebuild, and push forward after adversity.
- **E**xploration – The willingness to embrace curiosity and expand perspectives.
- **A**daptability – The flexibility to adjust when circumstances shift unexpectedly.
- **M**otivation – The internal drive that sustains us through long-term growth and change.

Dreams, Stories, and the Power of a Durable Mind

At its core, developing a durable mind is about rewriting the way we engage with our own dreams. Dreams are not just aspirations; they are the stories we tell ourselves about who we are, what we are capable of, and what is possible for our future. When we dream with determination, resilience, exploration, adaptability, and motivation, we don't just *wish* for a better life—we take active steps to shape it.

But here's the challenge: just as stories have plot twists, our dreams often encounter obstacles. The path is rarely linear, and durability is required to navigate those moments when things don't go as planned. A durable mind doesn't crumble in the face of adversity—it learns, adjusts, and keeps moving forward.

Why Stories Matter

What makes us give up on ourselves so easily? I realized that the promise I had made to myself was merely a goal, but what I needed was a standard. By definition, a goal is the object of our ambition and effort toward a desired result. A standard, on the other hand, is an established norm or way of doing things against which all other decisions and outcomes are measured. A standard isn't just a dream to be achieved; it's a system for evaluating the value of choices and their consequences. When I made that promise to myself, it was a goal. What I needed now was to establish it as a standard, and that required a cognitive investment rooted in durability and toughness.

What does it mean to have mental toughness, and why is it important to a resilient life? Mental toughness can be defined as having a psychological edge that helps you cope better with the difficulties and challenges of life. According to BetterUp, mental toughness is "the cognitive and emotional skill of reframing negative thoughts and adverse circumstances" (Cooks-Campbell, 2022). This highlights the actionable nature of resilience as a skill that can be developed through intentional practice. This is learned resilience. If resilience can be learned, then it must be a skill. Skills can be taught, learned, and practiced to be maintained. Just like the body, the mind requires training to sustain focus, determination, and confidence in the face of adversity and success. Our minds are a resource to help us accomplish things, build and maintain relationships, and solve problems. If you're not thinking critically, you're likely being led by your emotions, which can be dangerous. When someone says, "follow your heart," it doesn't mean to ignore your thinking and act purely on feelings. Instead, it's an admonition to pay attention to your "why" instead of just the "what" of your goals, hopes, and dreams. Developing habits that cultivate a durable mind is essential to accomplishing your "why".

Mental toughness, like any skill, must be nurtured through consistent practice. Just as physical training strengthens the body, mental exercises help build the resilience necessary to face life's inevitable challenges. But where do we begin cultivating these habits of mind? One powerful method is through storytelling. Stories have long been a means of imparting wisdom and shaping our understanding of the world. Children's books offer simple yet profound lessons that resonate with people of all ages. After spending most of my career as both a professional mental health practitioner and educator, I became fascinated by the lessons in children's books and used them to engage my students and audiences. An epiphany brought me to the realization that adults still needed the lessons these books offered. This led me to launch a podcast using the format of reading children's picture books and extrapolating themes and meaning from the stories. The lessons learned had such an impact on me and my audience that I decided to capture them in this book.

Each chapter is formatted to include the name of the children's book, the author, a summary of the story, the lessons learned, and suggestions or reflections to help form the habit of developing a durable mind. Many thanks to the authors of these stories and their contributions to this conversation. Throughout the book, you will also find sections called *The Durability Lab,* which offer strategies, exercises, and reflection prompts designed to help you actively engage with the lessons.

The Durability Lab is unique because it:

- Uses storytelling to teach complex concepts in relatable ways.
- Provides interactive exercises that reinforce mental habits.
- Encourages flexibility and growth, helping readers adapt strategies to their unique challenges.
- Focuses on mental durability, emphasizing progress and transformation rather than perfection.
- Promotes personal reflection, ensuring each reader's journey is deeply personal and impactful.

The focus of these labs is on helping you develop resilience and flexibility in your actual life, not on theoretical concepts. By practicing the principles and engaging in these labs, you'll embark on a journey toward a more settled, steady, and resilient way of living.

So, I invite you to approach this book with curiosity and openness. Let these stories and exercises challenge your thinking, inspire self-reflection, and guide you toward developing a durable mind. Your journey toward resilience begins here—step into it fully and discover the strength within you.

KEY #1: DETERMINATION

Building the Foundation for Growth

Determination is not just about pushing through obstacles, it is about forging meaningful connections and setting realistic yet ambitious expectations for ourselves. In Chapter 1, we explore how relationships and connections play a crucial role in shaping our resilience. True determination is not a solitary endeavor; it is strengthened by the support, encouragement, and accountability of others. Building a durable mind requires a willingness to lean into relationships that challenge and uplift us.

In Chapter 2, we examine the impact of expectations—both our own and those placed upon us. Determination requires managing expectations in a way that fosters growth rather than discouragement. When expectations are too rigid, they can create frustration and self-doubt, but when approached with flexibility and self-awareness, they become a tool for motivation and achievement. Together, these chapters reveal that determination is not just about persistence, it is about setting the right foundation through meaningful connections and well-balanced expectations that guide us toward growth and resilience.

Chapter 1: Developing Through Connection

"We are hardwired for connection, yet when we experience pain, we often armor up to shield ourselves. True resilience comes not from perfect protection but from the courage to let others help us heal." — Brené Brown

Introduction

In a world that often feels hostile and disconnected, it is easy to become defensive, build walls, and push others away. We convince ourselves that isolation is the best way to protect ourselves from further pain. But is that truly the path to peace? Inspired by the story *Nobody Hugs A Cactus* by Carter Goodrich, this chapter explores the dangers of living a life of isolation and the transformative power of connection. Building a durable mind does not happen in isolation. Emotional resilience and mental strength are often forged through our relationships with others and the connections we cultivate. When we effectively process our pain and open ourselves to meaningful connections, we strengthen not just our emotional well-being but our overall mental durability. Let us discover how connecting with others is crucial for developing a durable mind.

Book Summary

In *Nobody Hugs A Cactus,* we meet Hank, a grumpy and solitary cactus who takes pride in keeping others at bay. From tumbleweeds to cowboys, every passerby's cheerful greeting is met with Hank's annoyance and prickly attitude. Despite his insistence that he doesn't need anyone, Hank

begins to realize that his solitude feels more lonely than peaceful. It is only after a kind gesture from Rosie, the tumbleweed that Hank begins to let his defenses down, opening himself to the possibility of connection. Through Hank's transformation, the story beautifully illustrates the power of kindness, friendship, and the vulnerability and courage it takes to embrace change by letting others in.

Prickly Defenses – The Illusion of Protection

In *"Nobody Hugs a Cactus,"* we meet Hank, the protagonist in our story, who is a cactus and has mastered the art of keeping others at a distance. His sharp exterior mirrors his attitude, creating a barrier between himself and the world. Hank's irritability and defensiveness push away anyone who tries to connect with him, leaving him in a self-imposed isolation. Like Hank, many of us develop defensive behaviors as a way to protect ourselves from pain or vulnerability. These behaviors, whether irritability, aloofness, or a quick temper, act as shields against the possibility of being hurt. However, they also isolate us, preventing the meaningful connections we need to thrive. When unresolved pain leads us to build emotional walls, we may feel safe temporarily, but in the long run, we risk cutting ourselves off from the relationships that foster resilience and growth.

Hank is quick to take offense and has spent so much time pushing others away that he's created a life and disposition that is prickly. When someone is "prickly" they are ready to take offense and are looking for a reason to be offended. They are easily triggered and intentionally push others away in order to feel safe. At some point, we all encounter someone who seems guarded, difficult, or abrasive or perhaps we recognize these "prickly" traits in ourselves. Like Hank, people who exhibit defensive behaviors are often serious about keeping others at a distance, using these defenses as shields to prevent further hurt. While this might be a form of self-preservation, it often comes at a cost that isolates us from the connection and support necessary for growth and healing.

These "defenses" often develop in response to painful experiences that leave us feeling vulnerable. When life feels unpredictable or unsafe, we may become sensitive, irritable, or overly cautious, adopting behaviors that seem to protect our emotional or relational well-being. This can manifest as criticism, quick tempers, or emotional detachment—strategies designed to shield us from rejection or harm. However, these coping mechanisms often create patterns that cause the development of a life of disconnection and loneliness.

What causes this prickliness? Poorly processed pain is at the root of many unhealthy defensive behaviors. When pain remains unresolved, it can trap us in unhealthy cycles of thought and action, reinforcing behaviors that push others away.

Examples of how poorly processed pain can manifest:

- Hypervigilance
- Lack of trust
- Defensiveness
- Difficulty regulating emotions, especially anger
- Low frustration tolerance
- Control issues, to overcompensate for feeling helpless
- Perfectionism
- Clinginess

These defenses may provide momentary relief from vulnerability, but over time, they weaken us by cutting off access to the relationships and connections we need to flourish. For those seeking to develop a durable mind, it is crucial to recognize when these patterns are no longer serving us. Sometimes our systems of defense far outlive the seasons and conditions that required them for survival. Similar to Hank, we may apply outdated strategies to various situations by becoming entrenched in habitual modes of operation and misinterpreting them as self-care practices. True resilience comes not from avoiding vulnerability but from addressing our pain, breaking the cycles of defensiveness, and allowing space for authentic connection.

The Power of Connection in Building Durability

Hank's life is quiet and seemingly peaceful, but it is a lonely existence. Despite his best efforts to convince himself otherwise, Hank's solitude is not true peace. As defined here, peace is a state of flourishing, growing, and thriving in our relationships with ourselves and others. How much of it we experience is an indication of the wellness of the soul. The story illustrates that isolation, while it may feel safe, comes at a high cost. When we cut ourselves off from others, we also cut ourselves off from the very things that bring life meaning—connection, love, and growth. Hank's solitude is not sustainable because true peace cannot exist without connection. Our isolation might be misconstrued as peace due to its quietness. However, it is important not to equate quiet with peace, as a lack of engagement does not inherently lead to a peaceful state.

If you have ever told yourself that you do not need people, it is just not true. You may not need a lot of engagement with them, but you do need some for your soul to prosper, leading to mental, emotional, and relational health. Prosperity is not about money; it is about flourishing and growing strong. **Do not be in denial about your need for people!**

The challenge is to consider how your own unprocessed or poorly processed pain might be affecting the way you show up in the world. Developing a durable mind requires meaningful connections with others. Isolation may feel safe, but it often leads to emotional stagnation. Hank's journey in "Nobody Hugs a Cactus" is a powerful reminder that true peace and resilience come not from cutting oneself off, but from embracing vulnerability and allowing others in. Authentic connection brings peace—not the quiet solitude that Hank mistakes for peace, but the kind that stems from emotional wellness and healthy relationships. For anyone working to build mental resilience, processing pain through connection rather than isolation is essential. However, recognizing where pain exists in our lives is the first step toward healing. An emotional audit can help uncover areas of emotional or relational pain that may be holding you back. The following exercises are designed to increase awareness and provide tools for processing these experiences. If you discover deep-seated wounds, seeking professional support can be an important part of your healing journey. A durable mind isn't built by avoiding pain but by learning to process and grow from it.

The Emotional Audit (Identifying Pain Points)

- **Objective:** Assess current emotional triggers and patterns.
- **Instructions:**

1. Write down the last 3–5 situations that left you feeling deeply hurt, angry, or disappointed.
2. For each situation, answer the following:
    - What emotions did I feel?
    - Did the intensity of my response seem proportional to the event?
    - Have I experienced similar emotions in other situations?
3. Highlight any recurring themes or patterns.

- **Reflection Prompt:** What connections can you draw between these events? Could they be tied to deeper unresolved issues?

OR…

The Roots and Fruits Exercise (Tracing the Source of Pain)

- **Objective:** Trace emotional pain back to its roots and explore its impact.
- **Instructions:**

1. Draw a tree. Label the **roots** with early experiences that may have shaped your emotional responses.
2. Label the **trunk** with behaviors or patterns that grew out of those experiences.
3. Label the **fruits** with the consequences—positive or negative—of those behaviors.

- **Reflection Prompt:** What patterns or beliefs can you trace back to early pain, and how might they be influencing your present life?

Seeing Ourselves Clearly: Embracing Truth as the Path to Transformation

In the story, it is interesting that all the other characters (an owl, a rabbit, a cowboy, the coyote and Rosie the tumbleweed) all tried to positively engaged with Hank as they passed by and all seem to be going somewhere but Hank is symbolically and physically stuck in one place. The coyote is the first character in our narrative that challenges Hank's prickly disposition. He informs Hank that he is prickly both on the exterior and on the inside. This moment of truth-telling makes Hank uncomfortable, but it raises awareness, which is the first step toward any progress. Transformation, as Hank discovers, begins with the ability to hear and accept the truth. It is about acknowledging that our shields, although protective, are also impediments to the very things we require the most—love, connection, and peace.

The path to mental durability frequently begins when someone has the courage to be honest about how we are perceived by others, more importantly how they are experiencing us. Being taught unpleasant facts about ourselves is painful, but it is vital for progress. Having the courage to confront these realities, think through them, and make the required adjustments is essential to developing a durable mind. Like Hank, we occasionally need others to show us what we are unable to perceive in ourselves. Over time, resilience is developed via this kind of relationship, which is based on honesty and trust.

Another part of our transformation involves us coming to realize that our isolation is not accomplishing for us what we thought it would. For Hank, the journey towards connection continues with a small, seemingly insignificant act—the removal a cup that has been blown onto his face. This act, performed by Rosie, a compassionate tumbleweed, symbolizes the next step of Hank's internal transformation. His perspective, both literally and figuratively, begins to shift and he opens up enough to offer something of himself, a flower. By allowing himself to give and receive, Hank begins to experience the benefits of connection.

Similarly, the journey to developing a durable mind involves a shift in our perceptions that assists us in moving away from self-imposed isolation and toward meaningful relationships. These connections provide us with the strength to weather life's storms and the mental flexibility to adapt and grow. We all need people who are willing to see beyond our prickles and help us remove the "trash" that keeps us from connecting with others. These are the people who show up in our lives with kindness, patience, and compassion, even when we do not deserve it. Their acts of kindness open our hearts to the possibility of connection. Emotional connection is a resource that strengthens our mental resilience and fortifies us against future challenges. This shift in mindset is a critical step towards a life of peace, connection, and durability.

Moving Beyond Defenses – Embracing New Connections

One of the most important lessons from *"Nobody Hugs a Cactus"* is Hank's gradual realization that perhaps connection is not as dangerous as he once thought. He moves from saying "I don't need anyone" to recognizing that "maybe a hug wouldn't be so bad." This shift is where we learn that just because we have not found peace or connection *yet* does not mean it is impossible. By embracing the idea of "yet" we give ourselves permission to grow beyond our defenses. Our willingness to connect helps us move past our fears and opens us to the support of others, reinforcing our mental strength. Mental durability is not about never needing others, it is about recognizing that connection, though sometimes uncomfortable, is necessary for our growth and prosperity.

Conclusion

Hank's journey is a powerful reminder that while defenses may offer temporary protection, they often become the very barriers that keep us from the peace and connection we truly need. In trying to shield ourselves from pain, we sometimes end up reinforcing the loneliness we were trying to avoid. True resilience is not built through isolation but through connection—through the willingness to be seen, to be supported, and to engage with others even when it feels uncomfortable.

The path to mental durability begins with awareness—the ability to recognize when our defenses are no longer serving us well. Hank's transformation from "I don't need anyone" to "maybe a hug wouldn't be so bad" highlights the power of shifting our mindset. Just because we haven't yet experienced deep connection or inner peace doesn't mean it's unattainable. A durable mind is not one that rejects vulnerability but one that understands the strength found in relationships.

We all need people who can see beyond our "prickles" and help us remove the barriers that keep us from meaningful connection. These individuals—whether mentors, friends, or community members—play a vital role in our growth and resilience. By embracing the idea of *yet*—that we are still evolving, still growing, still learning—we allow ourselves the grace to move forward. Mental durability is not about merely surviving; it is about thriving through connection, allowing ourselves to give and receive support, and cultivating relationships that strengthen us for the journey ahead.

For more insights and personal stories related to this chapter, listen to Episode 1 of The Life Sculptors Podcast:

- **Episode Title:** "Finding Peace Through Difficult Relationships"
- **Listen Here:** https://youtu.be/B54E-nQmhag

Durability Lab

Before diving into this first Durability Lab, remember that these sections are designed to help you apply what you've learned in each chapter. Each section offers strategies, exercises, and reflection prompts designed to help you cultivate the habits and mindsets necessary for resilience. Think of them as mental training grounds—opportunities to practice and strengthen your resilience. Approach each activity with curiosity and commitment, knowing that every step you take builds the foundation for a more durable mind. Just as we discussed in the introduction, durability is not built overnight—it grows through consistent practice, thoughtful reflection, and intentional effort. Use these tools to move beyond theory and start applying what you've learned to your daily life. The Durability Lab invites you to move from theory to practice. Dive into these exercises with curiosity and dedication, knowing each step builds the foundation for a resilient mind.

The Durability Lab: Exercises for Building Connection

1. **Mapping Your Support System:**
   - Write down the names of people you turn to for emotional, practical, or inspirational support.
   - Identify areas where you feel isolated and brainstorm ways to foster connections in those spaces.
2. **Daily Connection Challenge:**
   - For one week, intentionally engage with someone you care about each day. This could be a kind message, a shared activity, or simply listening without distraction.

Reader Exercise: The Wall Reflection Journal

1. **Identify Your Walls**: Take a moment to write down the ways you might be pushing others away (e.g., irritability, sarcasm, aloofness). Ask yourself: *What am I trying to protect?*
2. **Acknowledge the Cost**: Reflect on how these defenses might be keeping you from meaningful connection. Are they serving you, or are they creating loneliness?
3. **Take One Step**: Write down one small action you can take this week to open yourself up—like reaching out to a trusted friend, being kind to someone difficult, or letting someone see a softer side of you.

Chapter 1 Durability Reflection Questions

As you reflect on this chapter, consider how your relationships are contributing to your mental resilience. Embrace the truth, allow yourself to process your pain, and take steps towards a life of connection, where peace is found not in isolation, but in the warmth of meaningful relationships.

1. Are there areas in your life where you have built defenses to protect yourself from pain or vulnerability? How are these defenses impacting your relationships?
2. What small steps can you take to move away from isolation and toward meaningful connection with others?
3. Who in your life challenges you to see yourself more clearly? How can you embrace their honesty to foster growth?
4. Think of a time when an act of kindness helped you lower your defenses. How did this experience impact your perspective on connection?
5. How can you show kindness and patience to someone who may be building walls to protect themselves?

NOTES

CHAPTER 2: MANAGING EXPECTATIONS

"You can't stop the waves, but you can learn to surf." — *Jon Kabat-Zinn*

Introduction

A durable mind is not just built through overcoming obstacles such as poorly processed pain; it also requires mastering another aspect of our internal world, particularly how we manage expectations. Life is full of unexpected twists, and our ability to remain resilient is deeply connected to how well we can navigate disappointment and adjust to reality. In this chapter, inspired by *"When Things Aren't Going Right, Go Left"* by Marc Colagiovanni, we explore how managing expectations can help build a durable mind capable of facing uncertainty with strength and flexibility.

Much of our emotional turmoil comes from the gap between what we expect and what actually happens. This gap, if not handled carefully, can undermine our resilience, and leave us feeling frustrated or defeated. It is not just the external circumstances that challenge us; it is also how we internally respond to them. But what if we could change how we perceive and respond to these moments?

Book Summary

In Peter Reynolds' simple yet expressive illustrations, a small child is depicted walking down a road, shedding suitcases and other belongings along the way. Meanwhile, Marc Colagiovanni's clever wordplay speaks to a more mature audience, offering a deeper message about how life unfolds through abstract experiences. The narrative begins with, "One day, for no particular reason, nothing was going right. Absolutely, positively, NOTHING was going right. So...I decided to go left." This decision symbolizes the choice to let go of burdens, visually represented as tiny red monsters—anxieties, frustrations, and doubts. A suitcase full of jagged orange anxieties, a backpack of yellow frustrations shouting, "You can't do it!" and "Give up already!" and a bag of hairy green doubts are all left behind as the narrator faces a challenge. Yet, after taking the risk and realizing the power of changing direction, the once-menacing worries shrink, becoming so small that they can be easily picked up again—though the narrator now understands that going left made everything right in the end.

Our Expectations

In *"When Things Aren't Going Right, Go Left,"* the character faces a day where nothing seems to go right. Our typical response when things do not go as expected is to try and control people, places, and things. We are prone to try and control the way life goes so that we can obtain the safety and peace we desire. But this approach can result in us trying to force things to align with our expectations. Forcing the proverbial square peg into the round hole ultimately leads to attempts at changing what is beyond our control, when what we really need is to adjust our perspective. This shift in thinking mirrors the mental flexibility required for a durable mind, which allows us to adapt when things do not unfold as we expected.

How often do we experience moments or seasons in our lives when it seems like there is no rhyme or reason for the way things are happening? Things going "right" is not an issue of morality but more an issue of expectation. Expectations shape much of our emotional world and create mental pictures of how things "should" go. We set expectations every day, often without realizing it: expectations for how our day will go, how others will behave, or how certain events will unfold. (Brown, 2021) One day recently I had a "taste" for some fried catfish. I could smell it, see it with my mind's eye, and taste it too! All of our senses get involved when we have expectations. Got to the restaurant and I overheard a server tell another customer "Sorry, we are all out of catfish." I picked up my stuff and left the restaurant. I was disappointed. Maybe you have left work or school and "had a taste" for something you expected to be in the frig at home only to arrive to the realization that someone has eaten it! When things do not go as planned, our immediate reaction is often frustration, disappointment, or even despair.

Where do our expectations come from? What intel have we been consciously or unconsciously gathering that help us determine that things are going "right"? If we are unaware of how our expectations get set, then we will surely become victims of our own expectations because they have more than likely been built on things we cannot control. Here is what they can sound like in our heads: when our internal dialogues begin with "shoulds" and "aught to's" they are pointing to our expectations. Or we conclude that something is just plain common sense which is based on the assumption that everybody thinks like you or even worse that your way of thinking or feeling about something is "THE Right" way.

A durable mind is one that can withstand disappointment or difference without losing hope or momentum. The key to this is managing expectations in a way that keeps us grounded in reality while still remaining optimistic about the future. By learning to manage these expectations, we develop the resilience to bounce back from setbacks. Instead of clinging to rigid ideas of how life should be, we become more adaptable, allowing us to grow and thrive even in difficult and diverse situations.

The Role of Flexibility in a Durable Mind

Flexibility is essential for building a durable mind. In *"When Things Aren't Going Right, Go Left,"* the character learns that sometimes, the path forward is not about pushing through obstacles but finding an alternate route. This flexibility is not a sign of giving up, but of mental strength. It shows that we can adjust our course without letting disappointment or frustration derail us.

Our expectations often come with an emotional attachment. This attachment can make it difficult to let go when things do not go our way. However, developing a durable mind means learning to release those emotional ties and embrace flexibility. This does not mean lowering our standards or giving up on our goals, it means being open to different outcomes and recognizing that our durability is strengthened from how well we can pivot when facing the unexpected.

Another key to managing our expectations is learning to deal with the timing of things. Staying flexible in our prospects by adding the concept of "yet" can make a world of difference. When we encounter disappointment, it is easy to think in absolutes, "I'm not good enough," or "I'll never get this right," or "this always happens." But the power of a durable mind lies in adopting the mindset of "yet." Instead of saying, "I can't do this," we can say, "I can't do this *yet*."

This small but powerful shift in thinking allows us to remain hopeful and determined, as we navigate unexpected and sometimes unwanted changes or challenges. The "yet" mindset gives us permission to be in progress and reminds us that just because something has not happened *yet* does not mean it never will. This kind of mental endurance is essential for long-term growth and resilience. We will explore the concept of "yet" more in chapter 3.

Managing Self-Talk for a Durable Mind

Another critical aspect of managing expectations is how we talk to ourselves when things do not go as planned. Our ability to move forward is influenced by the words and voices we listen to, and it starts with our own internal dialogue. *(see figure 2.1 for examples)* The information we feed our minds about our circumstances matters. The person you talk to the most in your life is YOU. We have become so accommodating to our negative, defeating, and critical self-talk that we have normalized this internal mental and emotional environment created by our own words. Our thinking and feelings can be far more fragile than we are willing to admit. Evidence of our fragility is when we allow our thinking to become absolute: "Everybody hates me," "Nothing ever goes right for me," "It always happens to me"—"Every Time", "Never", "Always", "Nothing", "Ever" are words that are part of this verbal arsenal.

Instead of being overly critical or negative, it is more helpful to learn to adjust our thinking and focus on what is possible. Stop allowing your thoughts and feelings to go wherever they want to. You are not at the mercy of your thoughts and feelings. If you do not direct them, they will direct you! Changing directions in your thinking can make a world of difference. Sometimes you must decide to put down some of the baggage you have been carrying and stop hoarding negative thoughts and emotions. We struggle to let go of the feelings and thoughts associated with negative memories and situations from our past because we have built our identity around them. We are emotional and mental hoarders, using them as a means of security through predictability and our hoards are cluttering us internally so that it impacts our ability to see life and ourselves clearly.

Managing your self-talk is a skill that must be honed, in order to better manage our lives. This is an element of maturity. According to psychologist Eric S. Jannazzo Ph.D., maturity is the behavioral expression of emotional health and wisdom. (Jannazzo, 2019) Negative self-talk—such as telling ourselves we're failures or that things will never improve—weakens our resilience and is an expression of an unhealthy emotional environment. On the other hand, positive, constructive self-talk helps us remain hopeful and focused on the bigger picture. If we increase our maturity by learning to manage our inner dialogue, we can better manage our expectations and build the mental endurance needed to handle life's challenges.

Reframing Disappointment

Disappointment is an inevitable part of life, often tied to our expectations and desires. One of the most powerful tools for managing expectations through maturity is the ability to reframe disappointment. When things do not go as planned, the emotions that follow—frustration, sadness, and anger can feel overwhelming. However, reframing disappointment is a critical skill for developing a durable mind. Instead of allowing disappointment to consume us, we can choose to reframe it as an opportunity for growth and a new perspective which changes the energy around the situation and the chemistry in our brains.

In *When Things Aren't Going Right, Go Left*, the main character faces obstacles that disrupt his journey, forcing him to make a choice: remain frustrated or find another way forward. This mirrors the challenge we all face when dealing with disappointment. Self-regulation plays a vital role in how we manage these moments. At the core of many difficult emotions, such as frustration and anger, is an issue of control. While we cannot control the actions or responses of others, we can control how we respond, like the character, we can go left. Self-regulation is the ability to adapt to various situations while managing our emotions and behaviors. It involves flexible thinking, emotional management, and behavior control, allowing us to inhibit negative impulses and focus on long-term goals. This skill is not something we are born with; it must be cultivated through practice.

A crucial aspect of self-regulation is developing emotional granularity, which is the ability to differentiate between specific emotions. Dr. Lisa Feldman Barrett-professor of psychology at Northeastern University indicates that like an artist distinguishing between shades of blue—indigo, cyan, and azure—someone with high emotional granularity can recognize subtle differences in their emotions. This awareness helps the brain process sensory information more effectively, allowing us to choose the right response to situations. For example, instead of merely thinking, "This sucks," a more specific thought like, "This is frustrating to me," enables the brain to find a solution faster. By expanding our emotional vocabulary, exposing ourselves to new experiences, and interacting with people from different cultures, we can increase our emotional granularity and enhance our ability to self-regulate.

Emotional Granularity – Expanding Your Emotional Vocabulary

Basic Emotion	More Specific Emotions	Nuanced Variations
Happiness	Content, Cheerful, Proud	Fulfilled, Grateful, Hopeful
	Excited, Joyful, Inspired	Playful, Jubilant, Optimistic
Sadness	Disappointed, Lonely, Hurt	Isolated, Defeated, Grieving
	Heartbroken, Melancholy	Nostalgic, Heavy-hearted, Weary
Anger	Frustrated, Annoyed, Resentful	Irritated, Bitter, Outraged
	Furious, Agitated, Offended	Disrespected, Rigid, Indignant
Fear	Anxious, Nervous, Hesitant	Overwhelmed, Uncertain, Apprehensive
	Dread, Insecure, Startled	Vulnerable, Exposed, Alarmed
Love	Affectionate, Warm, Compassionate	Tender, Devoted, Protective
	Romantic, Grateful, Admiring	Passionate, Nurturing, Cherished
Guilt/Shame	Embarrassed, Regretful, Unworthy	Self-conscious, Exposed, Humiliated
	Ashamed, Hesitant, Hesitant	Inadequate, Defeated, Disgraced
Surprise	Curious, Amazed, Shocked	Intrigued, Incredulous, Dumbfounded
	Startled, Awestruck, Stunned	Inspired, Breathless, Disoriented

Chart 2.1

How to Use This Chart

- When experiencing an emotion, pause and try to name it more precisely rather than defaulting to broad emotions like "happy" or "sad."
- Recognizing emotional granularity helps communicate emotions more effectively in relationships and decision-making.

Conclusion

Managing expectations is one of the cornerstones of developing a durable mind. By learning to adjust our perspectives, embrace flexibility, and engage in positive self-talk, we can strengthen our mental resilience and approach life's challenges with greater confidence. Colagiovanni's story reminds us that when life's burdens feel too heavy, we do not have to carry them indefinitely. Sometimes, it is necessary to pause, reflect, and let go of the weight we have been carrying. Self-regulation and emotional granularity help us step back from the immediate intensity of disappointment and consider a broader perspective. Perhaps the life we have envisioned is smaller and less fulfilling than the one that awaits us if we make different choices. By reframing our disappointment and adjusting our goals, we may discover that the detours in life lead us to better destinations than we ever imagined.

Disappointments and setbacks are inevitable, but they do not have to derail us. With the right mindset, we can turn these moments into opportunities for growth and learning. As Colagiovanni writes, "When life's burdens start to feel too heavy, don't be afraid to put them down for a while." Sometimes, we need to step back, see beyond our immediate feelings, and embrace what our life could be, rather than clinging to what we thought it should be. By doing so, we build the mental durability to face challenges with resilience, flexibility, and hope.

For more insights and personal stories related to this chapter, listen to this two-part episode of The Life Sculptors Podcast:

- **Episode Title:** *"What To Do When Things Aren't Going Right."*
- **Listen Here:** https://youtu.be/P4oI9sjd8YI (part 1) or https://youtu.be/YqskKdRh0KA (part 2)

Durability Lab: Strategies for Managing Expectations

1. **Recognize the Source of Your Expectations**

Expectations often stem from personal beliefs, cultural norms, or past experiences. Reflect on where your expectations originate and consider whether they are realistic or based on factors beyond your control. Awareness is the first step in managing expectations effectively.

2. **Reframe Disappointment**

Disappointment is an inevitable part of life, but it doesn't have to derail us. Instead of viewing setbacks as failures, see them as opportunities for growth. For example, if a job interview doesn't lead to an offer, consider what you learned from the experience and how it might prepare you for future opportunities.

3. **Adopt a "Yet" Mindset**

When things don't go as planned, it's easy to think in absolutes: "I'll never succeed" or "This always happens to me." Replacing these thoughts with "yet" statements encourages resilience. For example, "I haven't succeeded yet" shifts the focus from finality to possibility.

Readers Exercises:

The Expectations Review

1. Identify a recent situation where your expectations were not met. Write down what you expected versus what actually happened.
2. Reflect on how you reacted emotionally and mentally. Did you feel frustrated, disappointed, or stuck?
3. Consider how you might reframe the situation. What lessons can you take from it? What opportunities might it present?
4. Practice shifting your language. Replace absolute thoughts ("This always happens") with more balanced statements ("This happened, and I can learn from it").

The Power of Yet

1. Write down three areas where you feel stuck or unsuccessful.
2. Next to each area, add the word "yet." For example, "I haven't achieved my goal…yet."
3. Reflect on how this small change in language influences your mindset and motivation.

Chapter 2 Durability Reflection Questions

As you reflect on this chapter, consider how your expectations shape your emotional responses to challenges. Are there areas where you can adjust your expectations to foster greater resilience? How might adopting a "yet" mindset help you navigate disappointments and setbacks? Remember, developing a durable mind is about learning to adapt, grow, and thrive in the face of uncertainty.

1. How do you typically respond when life does not go as planned? Are there specific patterns of frustration or disappointment that emerge? What strategies could help you manage your expectations and approach setbacks with greater flexibility?

2. Reflect on your self-talk during moments of disappointment or failure. How might you replace negative or absolute thoughts ("never," "always," "nothing") with words that encourage growth and flexibility?

3. In what ways could adjusting your goals or reframing disappointment open up new possibilities in your life? Are there areas where a broader perspective might lead to a more fulfilling path?

4. How might practicing self-regulation and developing emotional granularity (learning to name your specific emotions) help you respond to disappointment more effectively? What new words could you add to your emotional vocabulary to describe how you feel?

5. What does the idea of embracing "what life could be" rather than "what life should be" mean to you? How might adopting this mindset strengthen your resilience and mental durability?

NOTES

The **Durability Lab Milestones** are designed to help you track your progress, stay accountable, and celebrate your wins as you work through the strategies and exercises in each chapter. Think of these milestones as markers on your journey, providing structure and encouragement along the way. These milestones aren't just tasks to check off—they're tools to help you build habits that foster resilience, adaptability, and mental toughness. Use them as guideposts to measure growth and stay committed to developing the durable mind you're working toward.

DURABILITY LAB MILESTONE #1

Determination – Building the Foundation for Growth

Determination is the fuel that keeps us moving forward, even when challenges arise. It is not just about pushing through obstacles but about staying committed to the process of growth. In the first two chapters, we explore the role of connections and expectations in shaping our ability to persevere. A strong support system and realistic yet ambitious expectations serve as the foundation for lasting determination.

To strengthen your determination, engage fully with the Durability Lab Milestone #1. This milestone is designed to help you stay accountable and track progress as you apply the exercises in this section. Determination is not just about endurance—it is about consistency. By committing to this process, you reinforce the habits that will sustain you when faced with adversity.

Progress Tracker

🔑 **Marker:** Below is a checklist you can use for each chapter's exercises to visually track your completion.

✓ Completed the reflection questions.

✓ Practiced the suggested strategy for 3 consecutive days.

✓ Shared insights with an accountability partner.

Weekly Check-Ins

Regularly checking your progress can build consistency.

🔍 **Marker**: Evaluate progress every 7 days using prompts like:

What changes am I noticing in my mindset?

What's been most challenging about this process?

What's one area I still need to focus on?

KEY #2: RESILIENCE

Resilience – Rising Strong Through Challenges

Resilience is the ability to withstand difficulties, recover from setbacks, and keep moving forward with strength and wisdom. A durable mind is not one that avoids hardship but one that learns from it, adapts, and grows.

In Chapters 3 and 4, we explore how emotional resilience and navigating adversity are critical in developing a durable mind. Emotional resilience allows us to process difficult emotions in a way that fosters growth rather than discouragement. Navigating adversity teaches us how to face challenges head-on, using both internal strength and external support to push through.

As you move through this section, remember that resilience is not just about bouncing back, it's about moving forward with greater clarity and confidence. The Durability Lab Milestone #2 will help you track your progress, develop self-awareness, and refine the tools you need to maintain resilience in the face of life's difficulties.

CHAPTER 3: THE POWER OF PATIENCE

"Patience is not the ability to wait, but the ability to keep a good attitude while waiting." — Joyce Meyer

Introduction

Patience is a critical but often overlooked aspect of mental resilience. In a world that demands instant results, the ability to wait, persevere, and trust in the process can be difficult to cultivate. Sometimes when we are waiting or want something to happen, it seems like it is happening for everyone else around us without much effort or time. Through the lens of comparison, other people make things look easy. When you let your emotions take the lead instead of your determination and identity, you may end up quitting out of frustration. If you are not careful you will apply permanent solutions to temporary problems. Sometimes it is easier to quit than it is to wait, but the long-term costs are just more waiting because you end up prolonging the inevitable.

Imagine a gardener tending to a sapling. Day after day, they water it, protect it from harsh weather, and ensure it gets enough sunlight. Despite their diligent care, the sapling doesn't grow overnight. Its progress is slow, often imperceptible, but the gardener trusts the process. Over time, the sapling transforms into a sturdy tree, its strength rooted in patience and consistent care. Like the gardener, cultivating resilience requires patience—trusting in the journey, even when progress feels slow. Patience is an essential component of a durable mind, giving us the endurance to face abiding challenges. In this chapter, inspired by "The Magical Yet" by Angela DiTerlizzi, we explore how patience, paired with hope and the belief in possibility, plays a vital role in developing mental durability.

Book Summary

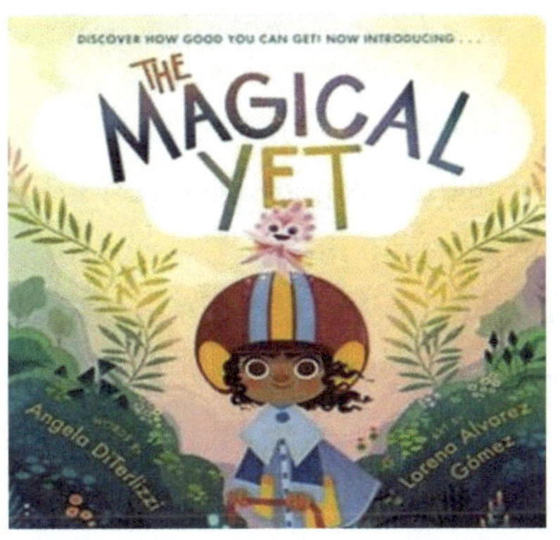

The Magical Yet by Angela DiTerlizzi is an inspiring picture book that encourages children to embrace challenges and keep trying, even when things seem difficult. The story introduces a magical creature called the "Yet," which symbolizes the idea that, although we may not be able to do something yet, we can achieve it with perseverance and practice. As the protagonist faces various obstacles, the "Yet" helps them understand that mistakes and setbacks are part of the learning process. The book's uplifting message about growth, determination, and the power of "yet" is beautifully paired with Lorena Alvarez's vibrant illustrations.

Patience as an Active Skill

In *"The Magical Yet,"* the author introduces the idea that we may not have achieved something *yet,* but that does not mean we will not in the future. This concept encourages us to see each step as part of a journey, rather than focusing solely on the destination. The "Yet" teaches us patience by reminding us that success, growth, and change take time. However, patience is not passive; it requires mental resilience and persistence. When we adopt the "yet" mindset, we allow ourselves to grow into our goals, recognizing that the process itself is valuable.

Patience is the active skill of being able to tolerate discomfort and uncertainty, trusting that with persistence, we will eventually achieve what we are working toward. It is often misunderstood as simply waiting, but it is much more than that. It is an active skill that requires us to manage our emotions, stay focused on the bigger picture, and navigate setbacks without losing hope. Another consideration of what patience means is to think through things so that you do not expect something that may be rightfully due to you, simply because you are experiencing provocation by difficulty.

Here is an example: If I am in line at the grocery store and it is taking longer than anticipated I might get impatient. Especially if people in other lines seem to be exiting faster than my line. And do not let someone need a price check on an item! Our patience is a measure of the resources we have allotted for certain things to get done. When something exceeds the amount of patience we originally allocated to the thing, we can become impatient. The journey to achieving their dreams is filled with challenges, but those challenges are part of the process.

"Yet" symbolizes the gap between where we are and where we want to be—and it is within this gap that patience becomes crucial. The work of patience is about staying committed, even when progress seems slow. A durable mind recognizes that setbacks and delays do not mean failure, nor do they mean it is never going to happen; they are simply part of the path to success. Patience allows us to remain grounded and focused, trusting that our efforts will eventually lead to growth, even if the results are not immediate.

Building Resilience Through Patience (Emotional Regulation is a tool of patience)

Patience strengthens resilience by helping us navigate life's inevitable delays and disappointments with grace. The implications of grace are that we learn to move steadily and with effective emotional regulation as we encounter setbacks or struggle. It is easy to become discouraged or frustrated, however, by practicing patience, we develop the ability to stay calm and composed, even when things do not go according to plan. This emotional regulation, the ability to control your thoughts, emotions, actions, and words, is essential for building mental durability and overall wellbeing.

Dysregulation can occur when we feel entitled. The current social environment has created a pace and readiness of the things we want in life such as we believe that if it does not come to us when we want it, life is somehow withholding what we are owed or deserve. Our prerogative if not checked by reality will have us believing that we have a right to everything we want. It is the psychological posturing of superiority that has us thinking we should not have to wait for something. The algorithm of our lives conditions us to believe that things "SHOULD" happen for us sooner or more quickly than is beneficial to our souls.

Just because you have a right to something does not mean that it is beneficial to you. It may even be beneficial for someone else but that does not mean it will have the same result or effect for you.

In *"The Magical Yet,"* the main character learns frustrations are temporary and that patience, paired with persistence, will help with goal achievement. This lesson mirrors the reality of personal growth in that success rarely happens overnight, but those who are patient and persistent build the resilience needed to achieve their dreams. Our impatience can lead to conflict, unhappiness, disappointment, depression, dissatisfaction, anger, and host of other negative emotions and mental states because we underestimate how long it will take to complete something, or we overestimate our ability to accomplish something quickly. This all speaks to our orientation about how we believe life ought to go. Lastly, our impatience is also an issue of dependency. We do not like depending on others because it opens us to being vulnerable. Our sense of agency, the ability to exert our own power to accomplish things, can get skewed especially when the significant adults in our lives were not as responsive as they needed to be for our own healthy development.

The critical or absent voices from the relationships in our lives (past and present), along with our own inner critic create noise that distracts us from persisting. Improving the skill of patience will strengthen our volition and decrease our orientation towards a victim mindset which can leave us feeling like life owes us for all the things we have been through. The skill of patience gives us a greater sense of freedom because we are not being controlled by our emotions or being held hostage by unhealthy expectations. Patience helps us pace ourselves, preventing burnout and allowing us to approach challenges with a clear and steady mindset. By learning to wait, to endure, and to trust the process, we develop a durable mind that can withstand setbacks without losing hope.

"*Patience is not waiting. It is understanding*." Brittany Josie.

Patience is not just about waiting for external outcomes, but also about being patient with ourselves. Developing a durable mind requires self-compassion, especially when we encounter challenges or make mistakes. In *"The Magical Yet,"* the characters learn to be patient with their own progress, understanding that growth takes time and that they are still learning. When we are patient with ourselves, we give ourselves the grace to grow, learn, and improve at our own pace. This self-compassion is essential for mental durability because it prevents us from being overly critical or discouraged when we do not achieve our goals as quickly as we would like.

The Role of Hope in Patience

Hope is an essential component of patience. Without hope, it is difficult to maintain the belief that our efforts will eventually pay off. It is embodied in the concept of the "Yet," reminding us that our current struggles are not permanent and that we can achieve more with time and effort. It is our hope that fuels our resilience by keeping us focused on what is possible, rather than what seems impossible at the moment. When we maintain hope, we are more likely to stay patient and persistent, even in the face of setbacks. Holding onto hope, however, is sometimes easier said than done. How do we stay hopeful when our experience does not align with our expectations?

1. Count the cost of what you are hoping to accomplish so that you can allot the mental, emotional, psychological, and relational resources necessary for achievement.

2. Narrow down your options. Too many choices make it difficult to choose and can lead to regret and confusion.

3. Be willing to change courses when something is leading nowhere. This is an adaptability skill that allows course corrections.

Hope is not the same as optimism. Hope is based on faith and belief in a positive outcome in the future, while optimism is based on the good that has already happened in the past supporting an expectation that good things will happen. So, holding onto hope is a key to developing a durable mind. It is this hope that keeps us moving forward, even when progress is slow or the path ahead is unclear. Hope makes room for us to get warmed up to the idea of the thing we want to accomplish. It knows that we will need to fix something, and that mistakes and failures are necessary parts of the learning and growing and capacity building. Hope ensures us that we get to stop and start over but we don't get to quit. Yet is pregnant with what is possible, and hope is the midwife to our dreams.

The Comparison Trap: How It Undermines Hope

A durable mind relies on hope as a stabilizing force—the belief that our circumstances can improve, that our efforts matter, and that better days are ahead. However, when we allow comparison to shape our perspective, hope can quickly fade. Social media and peer relationships, while offering some sense of connection and inspiration, often become avenues for unhealthy comparisons that erode our sense of possibility and progress.

Scrolling through social media, we are inundated with images of carefully curated lives—vacations, promotions, milestones, and picture-perfect moments. These glimpses, often devoid of struggle or imperfection, create the illusion that everyone else has it all figured out. In contrast, our own messy realities can feel inadequate, leading to discouragement and self-doubt. Instead of fostering hope and durability, this cycle reinforces feelings of failure, fragility, and stagnation.

The Scarcity Mindset

Social platforms thrive on instant feedback—likes, shares, and comments—that often serve as modern markers of approval. When our sense of worth becomes tethered to these metrics, hope shifts from being an internal conviction to an external competition. We begin to question our value, allowing comparisons to determine what's possible for us rather than focusing on our own unique journeys and timelines. Ultimately, this can lead to a scarcity mindset: the belief that success, happiness, and fulfillment are limited resources. When we view others', accomplishments as diminishing our own, we lose sight of abundance and opportunity. Instead of seeing someone else's success as proof that growth is possible, we interpret it as evidence that we've fallen behind, weakening our motivation and sense of hope. This mindset compromises mental durability, making it difficult to remain grounded in our intrinsic worth.

The noise of social media often amplifies a key component of the scarcity mindset which is the fear of missing out. Seeing others celebrate achievements or experiences can create anxiety about being left behind or excluded. This reinforces a focus on what we lack, rather than what we already have or what is within our control to change. Over time, this fixation on "not enough" can drain the energy needed to move forward.

Building Durable Hope

The antidote to comparison's corrosive effects lies in cultivating mental durability, the ability to remain steady, adaptable, and hopeful even when faced with external pressures. By anchoring our sense of worth in internal values rather than external validation, we reclaim ownership of our story and strengthen the foundation of hope and resilience. A durable mind doesn't measure itself against others' highlights. Instead, it focuses on progress over perfection and growth over comparison, recognizing that hope is renewable when rooted in self-awareness, gratitude, and purpose.

Conclusion

One of the key takeaways from *"The Magical Yet"* is that patience helps us maintain a long-term view of our progress. When we focus too much on immediate results, we can become disheartened by delays or setbacks. However, by adopting a long-term perspective, we see that each step—no matter how small—is contributing to our overall growth. “Yet” calls us to get on the same page with our process. Will you give yourself permission to wait the assigned and necessary time to prepare you to occupy the dream with integrity, authenticity, and the capacity to handle the responsibility that comes with it?

A durable mind requires the ability to see beyond the present moment and recognize the bigger picture. Patience allows us to stay committed to our goals, even when the immediate rewards are not visible. It helps us build mental endurance to keep moving forward, trusting that with time, effort, and persistence, we will achieve what we set out to do. It requires mental resilience, emotional regulation, and the ability to trust the process, even when progress seems slow. In *“The Magical Yet,”* we are reminded that growth takes time and that patience, paired with hope and persistence, helps us navigate setbacks with grace.

“Yet” is potent and progressive. We often settle for good enough because we will not commit to what it takes to get really good at something. The goal is not to just get it done, but to become better and better. “Yet” will help you to see that one accomplishment opens you up to the other possibilities that await you on the other side of achievement. We are incapable of outgrowing our yet.

For more insights and personal stories related to this chapter, listen to Episode 8 of The Life Sculptors Podcast:

- **Episode Title:** "Why Waiting Is So Hard."
- **Listen Here:** https://youtu.be/5xLQb9IzL38

 Durability Lab: Strategies for Developing Patience and Resilience

1. **Reframing Delays as Growth Opportunities**

Delays and setbacks can feel frustrating, but they are often opportunities to learn and grow. Instead of viewing them as obstacles, consider what they might be teaching you. What skills are you developing during the wait? How might this period prepare you for future success?

2. **Practicing Mindfulness**

Mindfulness helps us stay present and manage impatience. When you find yourself feeling restless or frustrated, take a moment to focus on your breath. Mindfulness anchors you in the present moment, reducing the urge to rush or become overwhelmed.

3. **Setting Realistic Expectations**

Unrealistic expectations can lead to impatience and disappointment. Break your larger goals into smaller, achievable steps. Celebrate these milestones as progress toward your ultimate goal.

Reader Exercise: The Patience Inventory

Create a "Patience Inventory" to help you reflect on and improve your patience. Divide a page into four sections:

- **Triggers:** List situations that make you feel impatient.
- **Responses:** Describe how you typically react in these situations.

- **Reframes:** Identify alternative perspectives or actions you could take to respond with patience.
- **Growth Areas:** Set one or two goals to practice patience in specific areas of your life.

Review your inventory weekly to track your progress and refine your approach.

Chapter 3 Durability Reflection Questions

As you reflect on this chapter, consider how patience plays a role in your own life. Remember, patience is not about waiting passively, it is about actively trusting that with time, effort, and perseverance, success is within reach.

- When you face setbacks or delays, do you find yourself focusing more on immediate results or on the bigger picture? How might adopting a long-term perspective change your approach to these challenges?
- What does "getting on the same page with your process" mean to you? How can aligning with your journey, rather than rushing through it, help you build resilience and integrity?
- In what areas of your life do you struggle with patience? How could practicing patience help you develop the capacity to handle the responsibilities that come with achieving your goals?
- Think of a goal you are working toward. Are you willing to give yourself the necessary time to grow into it, even if progress feels slow? What would it look like to fully trust the process?

- How does viewing "yet" as a powerful and progressive mindset inspire you to keep improving and exploring new possibilities? What role does patience play in helping you move beyond "good enough" to reach your true potential?

NOTES

CHAPTER 4: LEARNING FROM MISTAKES

"Every adversity, every failure, every heartache carries with it the seed of an equal or greater benefit." — Napoleon Hill

"Fall seven times and stand up eight." — Japanese Proverb

Introduction

Setbacks are an inevitable part of life, but how we respond to them defines our ability to grow and move forward. In "After the Fall" by Dan Santat, we are reminded that recovery is not only about mending what is broken, but also about discovering new strengths along the way. A reflection on the story of Humpty Dumpty, leaves us with some questions. Why was he on the wall to begin with? What kind of egg was he? He is the egg that is famous for falling but who knew that he got back up again! Humpty is an amazing example of resilience, but his identity is based on his fall. He reminds us that we all have a story and sometimes the details of our story get misconstrued depending on who is telling it and the motive and agenda behind why they are telling it. There is a story people tell about us, the story we tell others about ourselves, and the most important one is the story we tell ourselves about ourselves and these three are not always congruent. Part of the challenge for us is that we all have a story and the narratives we own and tell influence how we handle issues. The mistakes, accidents, situations, or circumstances of our lives do not have to become our identity. Mistakes happen, but we become what we say about ourselves as a result. These occurrences are not the end of our story but can serve as the beginning of us moving forward. The journey of redeeming resilience after failure or a setback is crucial in developing a durable mind. In this chapter, we explore how setbacks can become opportunities for growth and how getting back up after a fall builds resilience and mental durability.

Book Summary

After the Fall: How Humpty Dumpty Got Back Up Again by Dan Santat is a heartwarming picture book that tells the story of what happens to Humpty Dumpty after his famous fall. Humpty, once a lover of heights, is now afraid of climbing up high due to his traumatic experience. The story follows his journey of overcoming his fear and rebuilding his confidence. In the end, Humpty finds inner strength, and a surprising transformation occurs when he discovers his true potential.

Recognizing the Impact of Setbacks

In *After the Fall*, Humpty Dumpty's fall is more than just a physical accident, it has a deep emotional and psychological impact. His newly developed fear of heights, coupled with the resulting anxiety, exemplifies how setbacks can lead to feelings of insecurity and reluctance to attempt further endeavors. These fears—fear of failure, fear of being judged, and fear of experiencing the same pain again, can hold us back from returning to the lives we once knew. After experiencing failure, many of us feel reluctant to face similar challenges, worrying that we might stumble again. Self-awareness is crucial for understanding how setbacks affect us. This could include asking yourself questions such as,

- What has changed because of your missteps?
- Have you returned to where you were before the mistake, accident, or loss?

- What obstacles are holding you back from recovering fully—whether they stem from your own choices or the choices of others?

Our unwillingness to engage in deep reflection work could be a symptom of our fears. Negative emotions and irrational thoughts fueled by fears of being perceived as weak, incapable, or "broken" can lead individuals to avoid self-reflection due to the vulnerability it requires. Setbacks may shake our confidence and make us hesitant to take risks, but they also invite us to reflect, rebuild and grow stronger. By courageously facing our fears, we can discover new possibilities on the other side of our "fall."

An essential part of this reflective work is being open to our own vulnerability. While it may feel difficult to return to the life we once knew, perhaps it is not meant to go back to exactly how it was. We rebuild for better not to remain the same. It is through this vulnerability that we continue to build resilience. A consideration of the compassion we offer ourselves makes this possible. After a setback, it is easy to be critical of ourselves for failing or for not bouncing back quickly enough. However, as Humpty's story illustrates, recovery takes time, and it is important to be kind to ourselves during this process. By practicing self-compassion, we create an environment where we can heal and build our resilience without the added pressure of self-judgment. When we allow ourselves the grace to recover at our own pace, we foster emotional resilience and give ourselves the space to learn and grow from our setbacks.

Examining Resilience and Setbacks Across Generations

The way we process setbacks is deeply influenced by the generational context in which we were raised. Author/Speaker TD Jakes says, "You are born looking like your parents, but you die looking like your decisions." Our decisions are greatly influenced by the experiences we had growing up and how we processed them. The foundation for who we are gets established early and it takes great influence to become more, less or the same. Although we are raised by previous generations, as outlined in figure 1, each generation carries its own set of values, coping mechanisms, and responses to challenges, shaped by the cultural, economic, and societal conditions of their time. Bringing these influences under consideration can illuminate how our upbringing and social conditioning impact our ability to navigate setbacks.

Multi-Generational Interactions and the Connections to Durability

In multi-generational contexts, whether within families, teams, or communities, these differing perspectives on resilience can clash or complement one another. For instance, older generations may perceive younger individuals as less resilient due to their openness about struggles, while younger generations might view traditional stoicism as emotionally stifling. Bridging these gaps requires mutual understanding and a willingness to learn from each other's strengths.

These generational tendencies influence how individuals process challenges, build resilience, and support one another. Yet, no single approach is inherently superior. Instead, integrating these perspectives creates opportunities to foster collective resilience, where members of different generations learn from and complement one another. By recognizing the influences of generational contexts, we can better understand our own mental paradigms and build resilience by adopting practices from different perspectives.

Generational Perspectives on Resilience and Setbacks

Generation	Birth Years	Key Characteristics	Approach to Resilience and Setbacks
Silent Generation	1928–1945	Lived through economic hardship and war; focused on duty, discipline, and perseverance.	Often exhibit a "grin and bear it" mentality, emphasizing stoicism and self-reliance but less likely to show vulnerability.
Baby Boomers	1946–1964	Shaped by post-war optimism; value hard work, achievement, and stability.	Tend to view setbacks as personal challenges, relying on perseverance and work ethic, but may struggle with adaptability.
Generation X	1965–1980	Known as the "latchkey generation"; grew up with greater independence and skepticism toward authority.	Focused on self-reliance and practical problem-solving; adaptable but may hesitate to seek help or collaboration.
Millennials	1981–1996	Raised during rapid technological advances and shifting cultural norms; value collaboration and purpose-driven goals.	Open to seeking support and collaboration but may fall into the "comparison trap" due to social media pressures.
Generation Z	1997–2012	Digital natives; prioritize mental health, inclusivity, and transparency.	Embrace vulnerability and mental health conversations but may feel heightened stress from the public nature of setbacks.
Generation Alpha	2013–2025	Born into the digital age with AI and smart devices; global citizens aware of climate and social challenges.	Resilient through collaboration and technology use. Approach setbacks with emotional openness and reliance on digital tools for problem-solving. Likely to value collective solutions to challenges but may require support in developing critical thinking and non-digital coping mechanisms.

Figure 4.1

The Connection to a Durable Mind

Developing a durable mind requires acknowledging and leveraging multigenerational insights to build resilience. Understanding how each generation processes setbacks allows individuals to recognize how their generational influences shape their approach to challenges, shedding light on blind spots and revealing new opportunities for growth. Engaging with different generational viewpoints expands the tools available for navigating adversity; for instance, older generations often bring wisdom and patience, while younger ones contribute innovative strategies and technology-driven solutions. A durable mind thrives on connection, and fostering interdependence between generations creates opportunities for shared learning and mutual support, ultimately reinforcing both emotional and mental strength.

By weaving these perspectives into the process of developing a durable mind, individuals can navigate setbacks with greater adaptability, emotional intelligence, and collective strength. The goal is not to replicate one generation's approach but to create a synthesis that equips you to face challenges with resilience and grace.

Reframing Failure as Part of Success

One of the key lessons from *"After the Fall"* is that failure is not the end—it is a part of success. Success is not an event or a destination, it's a process that requires a commitment to investment. Humpty's fall could have easily defined his life, but instead, it becomes the catalyst for his transformation. He learns to fly, symbolizing his resilience and the growth that camc from embracing his mistake. Successful people often view failure as an integral part of their journey. They do not avoid it; they embrace it as a learning tool. A durable mind understands that every setback is an opportunity to refine skills, gain new insights, and build resilience. This mindset shift is what separates those who stagnate from those who continue to grow and evolve.

Reframing failure is a step towards rebuilding resilience after a setback and requires time, patience, and a willingness to keep trying, even when progress is slow. In "After the Fall," Humpty's recovery is gradual—he does not immediately return to the wall but instead takes small steps to rebuild his confidence. He starts with something simple: watching birds and thinking about what he once loved. Slowly, these small actions lead to bigger ones. Resilience is built through consistent effort over time. The process of recovery may not be quick or linear, but each small step forward brings us closer to healing and growth. A durable mind understands that setbacks are temporary and that with persistence, we can regain our strength and move forward. One of the most powerful messages of reframing is that setbacks can lead to transformation. The goal is not to just get back up but to transform into something greater than we were before; to experience brand new strength and freedom.

Humpty's journey highlights the power of persistence in overcoming adversity and its necessity to this process of reframing and recovery. Recovery from setbacks is rarely straightforward, yet the determination to face fears and rebuild leads to eventual success. Progress may be slow, and the road ahead may feel daunting, but continuing to move forward is essential to recovery. A durable mind embraces each step as one that moves us closer to growth and success, no matter the challenges along the way. Those with a durable mind understand that resilience is not about getting everything right the first time; it is about pushing forward, even when the path is difficult. By persevering, we learn that setbacks are temporary, and that consistent effort can help us rise again.

Conclusion

Learning from mistakes is one of the most important steps in building a durable mind. By reframing mistakes as opportunities for growth, embracing vulnerability, and persisting in the face of fear, we strengthen our resilience and become more capable of handling life's challenges. In *"After the Fall,"* Humpty's journey of recovery shows us that setbacks are not the end but pivotal parts of our growth. His fall could have defined him, but instead, it became the catalyst for transformation.

By embracing vulnerability, practicing self-compassion, and viewing failure as a step in the process of success, we can begin to build a durable mind. Recovery is not about returning to who we were before but about evolving into someone stronger and more resilient. Each setback, when reframed as an opportunity, brings us closer to the strength and freedom that comes from understanding and embracing our own journey. The key is to persist, to keep moving forward even when progress is slow, knowing that each small step contributes to our resilience and growth.

🎙 *For more insights and personal stories related to this chapter, listen to Episode 9 of The Life Sculptors Podcast:*

- **Episode Title:** "Mistakes Happen. Moving Forward Is A Choice."
- **Listen Here:** https://youtu.be/xGgVnUwf87o

 Durability Lab: Strategies for Embracing Vulnerability

1. **Acknowledge Your Defenses**

   Like Humpty's reluctance to climb again, our emotional defenses often stem from fear. Take time to identify the walls you've built—whether it's avoiding risk, suppressing emotions, or resisting help.

Awareness is the first step toward dismantling these barriers.

2. **Redefine Strength**

   Strength isn't about never falling; it's about the willingness to get back up. Recognize that showing vulnerability—whether by asking for help, admitting fear, or sharing your true feelings—requires immense courage and builds lasting resilience.

3. **Start Small**

   Humpty's journey begins with small steps, like observing the birds he once loved. Similarly, embrace vulnerability in manageable ways. Share a personal story, accept constructive feedback, or take a small risk. Each step reinforces your capacity for growth.

VULNERABILITY BLUEPRINT
01
ASSESS
Write down three areas in your life where you've avoided vulnerability (e.g., relationships, work, personal goals).
02
IDENTIFY
Identify one small action to take in each area that involves stepping outside your comfort Zone.
03
ACTION
Take action on the identified step.
04
REFLECT
Reflect on the outcomes. Did you feel stronger or more connected as a result?
05
REPEAT
Repeat this exercise periodically to track your progress and expand your comfort Zone.

Figure 4.2

Reader Exercise: Vulnerability Blueprint

Create a "Vulnerability Blueprint" to practice embracing openness:

1. Write down three areas in your life where you've avoided vulnerability (e.g., relationships, work, personal goals).
2. Identify one small action to take in each area that involves stepping outside your comfort zone.
3. Reflect on the outcomes. Did you feel stronger or more connected as a result?

Repeat this exercise periodically to track your progress and expand your comfort zone.

Chapter 4 Durability Reflection Questions

As you reflect on this chapter, consider how setbacks have shaped your own life. Remember, a durable mind is not one that avoids setbacks, but it is one that uses them as stepping stones toward growth and transformation.

- What story do you tell yourself about your setbacks, and how might reframing those experiences as opportunities for growth change your outlook?
- Are there fears or negative beliefs that have held you back from fully recovering after a setback? How could embracing vulnerability help you confront those fears?
- Think about a recent failure or challenge. What small steps could you take to rebuild your confidence and move forward in a way that supports your growth?
- What would it look like to view your setbacks as necessary parts of your success journey rather than as

obstacles? How might this mindset shift affect your persistence in pursuing your goals?

- How do you practice self-compassion during recovery, and how might giving yourself more grace improve your resilience? How might embracing vulnerability and persistence help you build a more durable mind?

NOTES

DURABILITY LAB MILESTONE #2

The **Durability Lab Milestones** are designed to help you track your progress, stay accountable, and celebrate your wins as you work through the strategies and exercises in each chapter. Think of these milestones as markers on your journey, providing structure and encouragement along the way. These milestones aren't just tasks to check off—they're tools to help you build habits that foster resilience, adaptability, and mental toughness. Use them as guideposts to measure growth and stay committed to developing the durable mind you're working toward.

"Yet" Progress Statements

Track shifts in your mindset by using "yet" statements.

🔍 **Marker:** Document personal "yet" statements like:

- I haven't mastered this skill—yet.

I'm still working through this fear, yet I'm improving each time

Resilience Vision Board

Use visuals to represent goals and intentions.

🔍 **Marker:** Revisit the board monthly to update images, quotes, or words that align with progress.

KEY #3: EXPLORATION

Unlocking Growth Through Curiosity and Discovery

A durable mind is not just about enduring challenges, it is about expanding possibilities. Exploration is the key to unlocking new perspectives, stepping beyond comfort zones, and embracing the unknown with curiosity and openness. The ability to explore—both externally in the world around us and internally in our thoughts and beliefs—fosters adaptability, resilience, and continuous learning.

In Chapters 5 and 6, we examine how curiosity and self-discovery shape mental durability. Compassion, as explored in Chapter 5, requires us to step outside of ourselves and consider the experiences of others, challenging our perspectives and deepening our connections. Chapter 6 builds upon this by emphasizing the power of curiosity in shaping how we respond to uncertainty, obstacles, and new opportunities. A curious mind does not resist change, it welcomes it as a chance to grow and expand.

Developing a durable mind involves exploring, asking new questions, and challenging old assumptions. Acts of compassion or curiosity-driven learning can facilitate this process. **Durability Lab Milestone #3** will assist you in evaluating how well you encourage exploration in your life and help you take intentional steps toward broadening your perspective. As you work through these chapters, you will navigate uncertainty and use exploration as a tool for growth.

CHAPTER 5: THE ROLE OF COMPASSION

"Compassion is not a relationship between the healer and the wounded. It's a relationship between equals." — Pema Chödrön

Introduction

Imagine a house with a cracked foundation. At first, the cracks seem small, barely noticeable. But over time, without repair, they grow deeper, weakening the structure. The same is true for our emotional well-being. Life's hardships, disappointments, betrayals, or failures can create fractures in our resilience. When left unattended, these emotional cracks can lead to deeper struggles, isolating us from connection and healing.

But what if, instead of ignoring the cracks or pretending they don't exist, we tended to them with care like a gardener who understands that growth requires both pruning and nourishment? Just as plants don't thrive under neglect, neither do people. We don't grow stronger from criticism, shame, or indifference. We heal when we are nurtured with compassion by ourselves and by others.

At some point, we all walk difficult roads, bearing burdens that are invisible to the outside world. If you've ever walked in a pair of worn-out shoes, you know how painful each step can be. Compassion is the practice of recognizing that pain, not dismissing it, not pitying it, but honoring it. It is the bridge between our struggles and our strength, allowing us to offer care, not just when it's easy, but especially when it's needed most.

Compassion is more than just kindness; it is a powerful tool that fosters resilience, strengthens connections, and helps us recognize hidden strengths in ourselves and others. In moments of challenge, compassion enables us to persevere through difficult circumstances, creating a durable mind that can withstand adversity. In this chapter, inspired by "Puppies for Sale" by Dan Clark, we explore how the practice of compassion—both toward ourselves and others—develops mental strength and resilience.

Book Summary

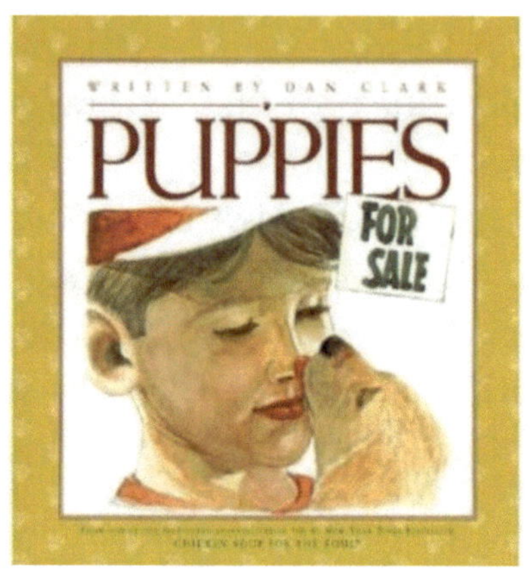

Dan Clark's "Puppies for Sale" is a kind and encouraging story about a small kid who picks a puppy with a damaged leg, just like his. The narrative focuses on concepts such as empathy, understanding, and overcoming challenges. The boy's decision to adopt the dog despite its physical limitations echoes his own journey and hardships, making it a moving narrative for readers of any age.

The Hidden Strengths in Our Vulnerabilities

In "Puppies for Sale," a young boy sees value in a puppy that others have rejected because of its lameness. The boy recognizes something in the puppy's physical vulnerability that resonates with his own experience, as he, too, has a leg brace. This mutual understanding highlights an important truth: our vulnerabilities, far from being weaknesses, can be the source of our greatest strength and empathy. A durable mind is not built by ignoring our vulnerabilities but by embracing self-compassion as a way to build resilience. By accepting our limitations and allowing ourselves to be imperfect, we strengthen our mental and emotional resilience. It is through this recognition that we can connect more deeply with others and find hidden strengths within ourselves.

Compassion as a Tool for Mental Fortitude

Compassion is not just a soft skill; it is a powerful force that helps develop mental toughness. When we practice compassion, particularly in inconvenient situations, we build emotional resilience by staying connected to our core values of empathy, kindness, and understanding. The boy in "Puppies for Sale" demonstrates compassion when he chooses the lame puppy, not out of pity, but because he sees the dog's worth beyond its physical limitations.

True compassion requires more than feeling sympathy for others—it involves taking action to support them. This active form of compassion helps build mental durability because it reminds us that we are capable of making a difference, even in the face of adversity. When we live and lead with compassion, we strengthen our sense of purpose, which is a key component of mental resilience.

The Role of Self-Compassion

Just as compassion for others aids in cultivating a resilient mind, self-compassion is equally crucial. The most prominent voices we hear are often our own inner critics. Frequently, we are our harshest evaluators, which can diminish our resilience and deplete our mental energy. However, by practicing self-compassion, we create an inner environment that fosters growth rather than self-doubt. Seeing yourself as a person worthy of compassion is essential to nurturing the ground of your heart to allow seeds of benevolence to be sown and grown on your own behalf. This is the benevolence we extend towards others.

In "Puppies for Sale," the boy's compassion for the puppy mirrors the self-acceptance he is learning to cultivate within himself. His leg brace does not define his worth, just as the puppy's lameness does not diminish its value.

Recognizing Lameness in Ourselves and Others

We often think about lameness in a purely physical sense, but there are many who experience lameness of the heart. The word lame can mean "not strong, good, or effective"—in other words, weak or ineffectual. At some point in life, all of us experience some form of lameness—whether it is emotional, relational, or psychological. Past wounds, betrayals, and failures can leave us feeling weakened, unsure, or ineffective in areas we once felt confident.

Sometimes, lameness looks like struggling to set boundaries in toxic relationships or feeling unqualified in a professional setting. It might mean being unable to resist the lure of gossip or allowing fear to keep us from pursuing our goals. Recognizing these moments in ourselves allows us to extend compassion to others who are experiencing similar struggles.

Compassion as a Pathway to Strength

Compassion is fueled by the understanding that we are all made of both strength and struggle. It is not about superiority or trying to fix someone else's situation, but rather about recognizing our shared humanity. True compassion does not come from pity, which is a near enemy of compassion—it comes from equity, the ability to see others as equals and honor their worth.

According to Gilbert and Choden (Choden), "With compassion, you have the wisdom to see and understand things as they are and feel motivated to do something about it." This means that compassion is not just a feeling; it is an action. It is the choice to extend kindness, understanding, and support even when it is difficult.

Barriers to Compassion: The Near and Far Enemies

In Buddhist philosophy, near enemies are qualities that resemble something good but ultimately work against it. For example:

- **Pity is a near enemy of compassion.** Pity subtly devalues another person because it creates emotional separation rather than connection.
- **Sameness is a near enemy of equity.** While it is comforting to believe that we all experience the same struggles, the truth is that each of us has unique challenges shaped by different life circumstances. Compassion requires acknowledging and honoring these differences.
- **Complacency is a near enemy of mindfulness.** Without mindful awareness, we can become numb to suffering—both our own and others'.

Far enemies, on the other hand, are direct opposites:

- **Cruelty is the far enemy of compassion.** It is an outright rejection of another's humanity.
- **Hostility is the far enemy of kindness.** It distorts righteous anger into personal attacks rather than focusing on the injustice itself.
- **Demonizing others is a far enemy of understanding.** When we allow pride or judgment to overtake us, we lose the ability to engage with different perspectives.

Recognizing these barriers is key to developing a durable mind. The ability to stay mindful, regulate emotions, and act with wisdom rather than reactivity allows us to cultivate true compassion rather than its near enemies.

This practice of seeing ourselves with the same kindness we extend to others is crucial for building a durable mind. Self-compassion allows us to recover more quickly from setbacks, approach challenges with patience, and maintain emotional resilience in challenging times.

Building Resilience Through Connection

Compassion also strengthens our relationships with others, which supports the role of community in fostering a durable mind. When we connect with others through acts of compassion, we create a support network that helps us navigate life's challenges. These connections serve as a source of strength, providing emotional and practical support when we need it most. This compassion fosters a sense of connection and belonging. Our own lameness, instead of being a barrier, becomes the foundation for a meaningful bond with others creating a greater sense of shared resilience and deepening our relationships.

The Resilience of Vulnerability

Demonstrating compassion requires us to take ownership of our own limitations and be vulnerable, which can feel uncomfortable, but vulnerability is a key component of mental resilience. Choosing each other, despite our limitations, shows a deep level of emotional strength. A willingness to embrace vulnerability can only come as we learn to accept our own. Vulnerability is often misunderstood as a weakness, but it is actually a source of strength. When we allow ourselves to be vulnerable, we open ourselves up to growth, connection, and healing. A durable mind is one that can face vulnerability without fear, knowing that it is through this openness that we build true resilience.

Conclusion

"Puppies for Sale" reminds us that true resilience is not about masking imperfections but embracing them as sources of strength. Compassion—both for ourselves and others—is a powerful force that fosters connection, healing, and endurance. It allows us to see beyond limitations, recognizing the inherent worth in each person and acknowledging that struggle is a shared human experience.

A durable mind is not built through isolation but through connection, understanding, and the courage to care. Compassion is not a sign of weakness; it is a testament to our resilience. It is the ability to stand in the face of pain, whether it is our own or someone else's, and choose to engage rather than retreat. By choosing compassion, we cultivate emotional flexibility, allowing us to withstand life's challenges while remaining open-hearted and present.

Compassion and wisdom must work together to create meaningful change. As you navigate your own journey, may you have the courage to extend the same grace to yourself that you offer to others. By integrating compassion into your life, you not only strengthen your own resilience but also contribute to a world where understanding, kindness, and shared humanity lead the way forward.

🎙️ *For more insights and personal stories related to this chapter, listen to Episode 6 of The Life Sculptors Podcast:*

- **Episode Title:** "Don't Be Lame. Be Compassionate."
- **Listen Here:** https://youtu.be/l7m-ihCi5fg

Durability Lab: Strategies for Cultivating Compassion

1. **Recognize Vulnerability as Strength**

   Just like the boy in Puppies for Sale, begin by acknowledging that imperfections are not weaknesses, they are opportunities to connect more deeply with others. Reflect on a moment when your own challenges allowed you to empathize with someone else.

   - Can you think of a time when you mistook pity for compassion?
   - Have you ever dismissed someone's pain because you assumed their experience was "just like yours"?
   - How can you practice compassion that is rooted in equity rather than superiority?

2. **Shift Your Inner Dialogue- Self-Compassion Check-In**

   Replace self-critical thoughts with compassionate ones. When faced with failure, ask yourself: "What can I learn from this experience?" instead of dwelling on what went wrong.

   - When was the last time you extended kindness to yourself?
   - What critical or judgmental thoughts do you frequently have about yourself?
   - How can you reframe these thoughts to be more compassionate?

3. Compassion in Action

Compassion is more than a feeling; it's a call to action. Engage in small acts of kindness, like listening to a friend or offering help to someone in need. Each act strengthens your ability to connect and builds mental resilience.

- Identify one person in your life who may be experiencing an unseen struggle.
- Choose a small act of compassion to extend to them—whether it's a kind word, an act of service, or simply holding space for their emotions.
- Reflect on how this act of compassion impacted both you and the other person.

Reader Exercise: The Compassion Mirror

Why Mirror Work?

Mirror work strengthens emotional durability by reinforcing positive self-talk and promoting self-awareness. It encourages you to face yourself honestly and celebrate progress, no matter how small. Through this practice, you build the foundation for a compassionate mindset that nurtures growth and resilience. This exercise is designed to help you build emotional strength and resilience by cultivating compassion—for yourself and others—through daily reflection and affirmations.

Step 1: Set Your Intention (Morning Affirmation)

Begin your day by standing in front of a mirror. Look yourself in the eyes and repeat one or several of the following affirmations, or create one of your own:

1. *"I am enough, and I am worthy of love and compassion."*
2. *"I give myself permission to grow through challenges and setbacks."*
3. *"I release judgment and embrace kindness toward myself and others."*
4. *"I see my vulnerabilities as opportunities for connection and growth."*
5. *"I am proud of the strength it takes to be gentle with myself."*
6. *"I will honor my progress, even when it feels small."*
7. *"I am learning, adapting, and becoming more resilient every day."*
8. *"I have the courage to face life's challenges with empathy and grace."*

Step 2: Weekly Review

At the end of each week, review your reflections. Look for patterns and growth. Ask yourself:

- How has practicing compassion strengthened my ability to handle challenges?
- In what ways do I feel more connected to myself and others?

Step 3: Adjust and Affirm (Optional)

If you notice areas where compassion is lacking, set new intentions for the next week. Add this affirmation to close your reflections:

"I am becoming stronger and more resilient by leading with compassion and grace."

Challenge:

Commit to practicing the Compassion Mirror exercise for 30 days. Track your emotional shifts and celebrate your progress along the way!

Chapter 5 Durability Reflection Questions

As you reflect on this chapter, consider how you can bring more compassion into your life. Remember, the path to a durable mind is paved with kindness, empathy, and the courage to embrace our vulnerabilities.

- How might embracing your own vulnerabilities as strengths change the way you view challenges in your life?
- When was the last time you practiced compassion toward yourself in a demanding situation? How did it impact your resilience and ability to move forward?
- Think of a time when you extended compassion to someone facing a challenge. How did this act of kindness strengthen your sense of purpose or resilience?
- What role does compassion play in your relationships? How might cultivating more compassion deepen your connections with others and build a stronger support network?
- In what ways can vulnerability be a source of strength in your life? How might accepting your own limitations open you up to greater resilience and growth?

NOTES

CHAPTER 6:
THE QUEST FOR CURIOSITY

"A mind stretched by new experiences can never go back to its old dimensions."

– Oliver Wendell Holmes Jr.

Introduction

Imagine standing at the edge of a forest, where two paths diverge. One path is well-trodden and predictable, while the other is overgrown, mysterious, and full of unknowns. The well-worn path feels safe, but it offers no surprises or new discoveries. The overgrown path, though intimidating, invites exploration and curiosity, revealing treasures and lessons for those brave enough to venture forward. Life's challenges often present these same choices: Do we stick with what we know, or do we embrace the unknown with curiosity and an open mind?

Curiosity is often seen as a whimsical or fleeting trait, but in reality, it is a powerful driver of growth and mental resilience. By embracing curiosity, we allow ourselves to explore new perspectives, adapt to change, and cultivate a durable mind capable of facing life's challenges with an open and flexible mindset. In this chapter, inspired by *"Knight Owl"* by Christopher Denise, we explore how curiosity, along with a willingness to venture into the unknown, plays a crucial role in developing mental flexibility and resilience.

Book Summary

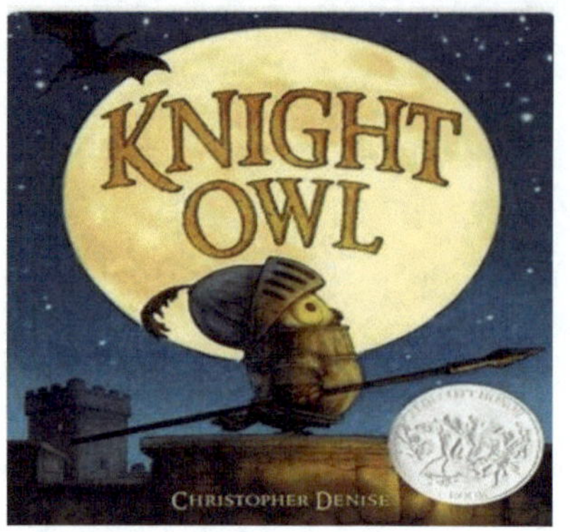

Knight Owl by Christopher Denise is a charming children's picture book about a young owl who dreams of becoming a knight. Despite being smaller and weaker than the other knights-in-training, Owl is determined to prove that he has what it takes. His courage and cleverness are put to the test when a dragon threatens the kingdom, and Owl uses his wits to outsmart the dragon, forming an unexpected friendship.

The Role of Curiosity in Mental Resilience

In *"Knight Owl,"* Owl's curiosity about the world of knighthood drives him to pursue a dream that others might consider impossible for an owl. His willingness to step outside the bounds of what is traditionally expected reflects the essence of mental flexibility. Rather than becoming stuck in rigid patterns of thinking, curiosity, as Owl demonstrates, fuels resilience by pushing us to explore new possibilities. Curiosity serves as a key to adaptability and growth. When we maintain a curious mindset, we are less likely to become entrenched in limiting beliefs or fixed ways of thinking. This openness allows us to pivot when faced with challenges and to continuously evolve, which is necessary to build a durable mind.

Owl's journey highlights the courage required to pursue curiosity, especially when it leads us into unfamiliar territory. He encounters fears and challenges along the way but continues to explore the unknown. This kind of courage is central to mental flexibility—it requires us to face uncertainty with the belief that we can handle whatever we find.

Curiosity is the fuel that propels us toward growth, learning, and adaptability. It challenges us to step beyond the familiar, seek out new perspectives, and remain open to possibilities. Just like *Knight Owl,* whose curiosity led him on a transformative journey, we, too, can develop resilience by embracing the unknown with wonder rather than fear. It also encourages us to view challenges as opportunities for learning, rather than as threats to our stability, which speaks to the importance of embracing discomfort in order to grow. A durable mind is not one that avoids uncertainty, but one that seeks it out as a way to build strength and adaptability.

The Power of Questions

One of the most important tools for developing curiosity is asking questions. In *Knight Owl*, Owl's journey begins with a simple yet powerful wonder: c*ould become a knight?* This single inquiry opens up a world of possibilities, sparking an adventure that builds resilience and confidence. Questions, even seemingly small ones, help us challenge limiting beliefs, unlock opportunities, and inspire growth. When we approach life with curiosity, we grant ourselves permission to explore, experiment, and even fail without judgment.

In her book, The Power of Wonder, Monica Parker says that *"Deeply curious people like to challenge themselves intellectually and thrive on unpredictability."* She goes on to reference some ways we can increase our curiosity such as seeking novel or newness and slowing down our lives, so we don't rust through exploration. (Parker) Curiosity is a key element of wonder which is necessary to help make us more compassionate and more open to new things.

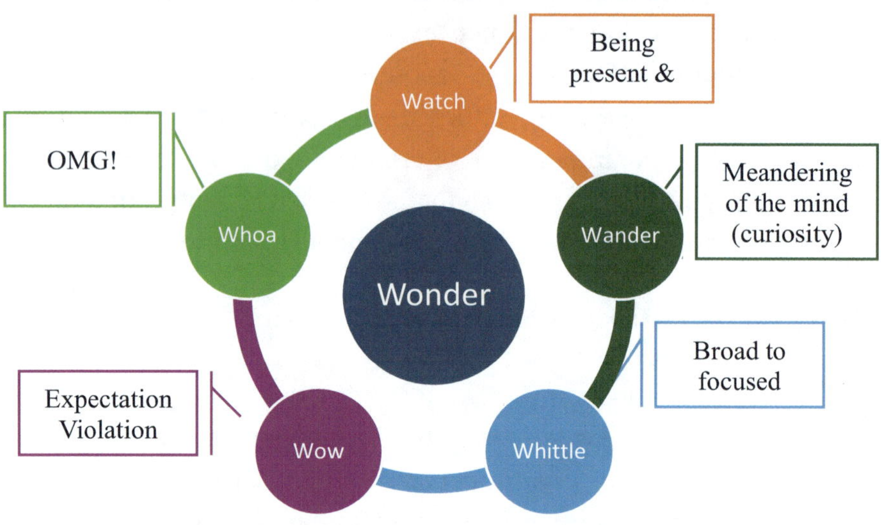

Figure 6.1
adapted from Wonder by Monica Parker

Much like Owl, many of us feel the urge to explore beyond what we know, and curiosity often serves as the spark for transformation. The questions we ask not only reflect where we are but also point toward what could come next. However, creating a safe space for exploration is vital because when we feel unsafe, questions can feel like accusations rather than invitations to learn. To foster growth, we must embrace questions as steppingstones to greater mental agility, insight, and personal development.

"The quality of your life will mirror the quality of the questions you ask yourself." —Kobi Yamada

Curiosity as a Path to Problem-Solving

Curiosity is not just about asking questions—it's about cultivating a mindset that welcomes uncertainty and explores challenges with an open heart. Studies show that individuals who maintain curiosity in difficult situations are more adaptable, better problem-solvers, and more likely to bounce back from setbacks. Psychologist Todd Kashdan, a leading researcher on curiosity, explains, *"Curiosity fosters resilience by keeping us engaged in the face of uncertainty. When we stay curious, we remain open to learning and adapting, which allows us to navigate adversity with greater confidence."* (Kashdan)

Our curiosity leads us to discover unconventional ways to succeed, despite the limitation's others might impose on us. The ability to think creatively and explore novel solutions highlights the connection between curiosity and creativity. Questions make room for innovative thinking, particularly when we encounter obstacles. Rather than becoming stuck in the problem, our curiosity through questions helps us shift our focus to potential solutions. By maintaining a curious mindset, we develop the mental flexibility needed to tackle challenges from multiple angles, increasing our chances of finding effective solutions.

Throughout history, some of the most successful and resilient individuals have used curiosity as a tool to overcome challenges:

- **Albert Einstein** was once told he would never amount to much because of his unconventional thinking. Yet, his relentless curiosity led to some of the most groundbreaking discoveries in science. His relentless questioning of the world around him led to groundbreaking discoveries in physics that reshaped our understanding of time and space. Instead of accepting conventional wisdom, Einstein's curiosity led him to reimagine the fundamental laws of the universe.

- **Oprah Winfrey** has used curiosity as a tool for transformation, both in her own life and in the lives of millions. Growing up in poverty and facing early career setbacks, she never stopped asking deeper questions about human experiences, emotions, and connections. Her ability to engage in meaningful conversations and seek wisdom from others helped her build one of the most influential media platforms in history.

- **Temple Grandin** a scientist and autism advocate, has used curiosity to drive innovation and resilience. Diagnosed with autism, she was curious about animal behavior, leading her to create humane livestock handling systems. Despite challenges, she asked questions and tested ideas, becoming a renowned expert in animal science and autism advocacy. Her story shows how curiosity can turn obstacles into opportunities.

These examples illustrate that curiosity is not just a trait but a skill that can be nurtured and used to build a durable mind.

Overcoming Barriers to Curiosity

While curiosity is a natural human instinct, many people struggle to embrace it due to barriers such as:

- **Fear of failure** – Worrying about making mistakes can stifle curiosity.

- **Perfectionism** – Wanting to have all the answers before taking action can limit exploration.

- **Fixed mindset** – Believing that intelligence and abilities are static discourages experimentation.

To overcome these barriers, we must reframe failure as a learning opportunity, remind ourselves that progress is more important than perfection, and adopt a growth mindset that sees every challenge as a chance to learn.

Building Confidence Through Curiosity

Curiosity does not just help us solve problems; it also builds confidence. Each time we try something new and learn from the experience, we strengthen our belief in our own abilities. This gradual accumulation of knowledge and experience fosters a sense of confidence that is rooted in resilience.

Confidence is built through action, and curiosity drives us to act, even when we do not know exactly how things will turn out. By embracing curiosity, we become more comfortable with uncertainty and build the confidence to handle whatever comes our way. Learning to trust yourself to sort through a variety of situations builds the confidence of a durable mind, one that trusts in its ability to learn and grow, even in unfamiliar circumstances. Our confidence in turn inspires confidence in others as we foster environments where others feel empowered to explore and share ideas. This builds collective resilience, as others around us learn to adapt and thrive through collaboration and exploration. A durable mind is one that seeks out knowledge not just for personal growth but for the benefit of others. Curiosity and confidence go hand in hand. When we allow ourselves to explore new ideas without fear of judgment, we build self-trust. A curious mind isn't afraid of failure—it sees failure as data, feedback, and an essential part of growth. This ability to detach from immediate outcomes and stay engaged in the process is what strengthens resilience over time.

Conclusion

The journey of the young owl in *Knight Owl* reminds us that curiosity is more than a fleeting interest—it is a powerful tool for building resilience and adaptability. By staying curious, we open ourselves up to new possibilities, creative problem-solving, and the courage to face uncertainty. Curiosity drives us to ask questions, explore unfamiliar territory, and build confidence in our ability to handle whatever challenges come our way. A durable mind is one that not only embraces curiosity as a means of personal growth but also encourages those around us to be open, collaborative, and adaptable. In the end, curiosity allows us to approach life with a sense of wonder and courage, helping us build a mind that is both resilient and open to continuous learning.

When we shift from a mindset of certainty to one of curiosity, we create space for growth, resilience, and deeper understanding. Just like *Knight Owl*, we discover new possibilities when we dare to ask, "What if?" Instead of fearing the unknown, we learn to see it as an invitation to expand our potential.

🎙 *For more insights and personal stories related to this chapter, listen to Episode 7 of The Life Sculptors Podcast:*

- **Episode Title:** "Who You? The Quest for Curiosity."
- **Listen Here:** https://youtu.be/6KYuM2Hm4dc

Durability Lab: Strategies for Cultivating Curiosity and Mental Flexibility

1. **Ask Open-Ended Questions**
   Practice asking, "what if" and "how" questions about challenges or goals. For example, "What if I tried a different approach?" or "How might I view this situation from another perspective?"

2. **Engage in New Experiences**
   Step outside your comfort zone by trying new activities or exploring unfamiliar topics. This broadens your understanding and sparks creative thinking.

3. **Adopt a Beginner's Mindset**
   Approach situations as if you're encountering them for the first time. This encourages you to see possibilities that may otherwise be overlooked.

Reader Exercise: Curiosity Map

Create a curiosity map to explore an area of your life where you feel stuck or uninspired. On a sheet of paper:

- Write your challenge or goal in the center.
- Surround it with questions like, "What new approach can I try?" or "What am I missing?"
- Add possible solutions or next steps to each question.
- Reflect on what patterns emerge. Are there recurring themes? Do some answers feel more actionable than others?
- Pick one action step and commit to trying it.

By visualizing possibilities, you develop strategies to move forward rather than remaining stuck.

- **Write your challenge or goal in the center of a blank page.** (Example: "How can I improve my confidence in public speaking?")
- **Surround it with open-ended questions, such as:**
  - "What is holding me back?"
  - "Who can I learn from?"
  - "What new approach can I try?"
  - "What am I missing?"

Curiosity Map Example 1: Improving Confidence in Public Speaking

Challenge (Center of the Map): *How can I improve my confidence in public speaking?*

Open-Ended Questions & Responses:

- **What is holding me back?** → Fear of judgment, lack of practice, past negative experiences.
- **Who can I learn from?** → TED speakers, Toastmasters, experienced colleagues.
- **What new approach can I try?** → Practice in front of a mirror, record and review my speeches, attend a public speaking workshop.

- **What am I missing?** → Feedback from others, breathing techniques for relaxation.
- **What's one small step I can take this week?** → Volunteer to speak in a small group setting.

✅ **Action Step:** *Join a local Toastmasters group and practice one speech per week.*

Chapter 6 Durability Reflection Questions

As you reflect on this chapter, consider how curiosity plays a role in your own life. Remember, a durable mind is one that remains open to the world, constantly learning, growing, and evolving.

- In what areas of your life could embracing curiosity help you move beyond limiting beliefs or fixed ways of thinking? How might this openness lead to new opportunities?
- Think of a recent challenge you faced. How could approaching it with a curious mindset have opened up different solutions or perspectives?
- What questions have you been afraid to ask about your own dreams or goals? How might exploring these questions with curiosity and courage empower you to act?
- How does building confidence through curiosity help you face uncertainty in your life? How might this confidence also inspire and empower others around you?
- What practices could you adopt to keep curiosity alive in your daily life, even when faced with challenges? How might these practices contribute to a more resilient and adaptable mindset?

NOTES

DURABILITY LAB MILESTONE #3

Strengthening Adaptability Through Reflection and Action

Adaptability is the foundation of a durable mind—it is what allows us to pivot when obstacles arise, adjust when circumstances shift, and remain open to growth even in uncertainty. This milestone focuses on **tracking progress, embracing flexibility, and learning from past challenges** to enhance your ability to navigate change with confidence.

The Adaptability Jar: Recognizing Growth in Action

Adaptability is built through **small shifts in thinking and behavior** that lead to lasting resilience. Create a visual representation of your progress by noting how you've **adjusted, pivoted, or changed course** when faced with a challenge.

Marker: Add at least one note per week to your Adaptability Jar.

- Write down a moment where you adapted to a new situation instead of resisting it.
- Include insights about how changing your approach led to a better outcome.
- Revisit these notes when you feel stuck to remind yourself of your ability to flex and adjust when needed.

The Challenge Log: Documenting How You Overcome Obstacles

Every challenge you face is an opportunity to fine-tune your adaptability skills. Keeping track of these moments will help you recognize patterns, build confidence in your ability to adjust, and develop new strategies for future hurdles.

🔑 Marker: Record specific obstacles and the strategies you used to overcome them.

- Describe a challenge that required you to shift your approach.
- Write down the strategies you used to handle it.
- Reflect on what worked and what you might try differently next time.

Why Adaptability Matters in Developing a Durable Mind

Life rarely goes as planned, but your ability to adapt determines your ability to thrive. By tracking moments where you successfully navigated change, you reinforce the mindset that challenges are not roadblocks—they are opportunities for creative problem-solving and growth. Use this milestone as a reminder of your ability to adjust, evolve, and keep moving forward.

KEY #4: ADAPTABILITY

Strength In Flexibility

A durable mind is not just about standing firm in the face of adversity, it is about knowing when to bend, shift, and adjust in response to life's challenges. Adaptability is a core element of mental durability because it allows us to respond to setbacks with creativity rather than rigidity, ensuring that obstacles do not stop our progress but instead refine our resilience.

Chapters 3 and 4 explore how adaptability strengthens a durable mind by helping us shift perspectives, reframe challenges, and take action even when the path forward is unclear. Feeling stuck is an inevitable part of life, but staying stuck is a choice. When we learn to embrace flexibility—both in our thinking and in our actions—we empower ourselves to navigate uncertainty without losing momentum.

This section will challenge you to examine where rigid thinking might be holding you back, encourage you to experiment with new approaches, and equip you with strategies to cultivate a more adaptable mindset. A durable mind thrives not by resisting change, but by embracing it as an opportunity for growth, learning, and transformation.

CHAPTER 7: GETTING UNSTUCK

"When we are no longer able to change a situation, we are challenged to change ourselves." — Viktor Frankl

Introduction

Feeling stuck is an experience we all encounter at some point in life. Whether it is in a career, a relationship, or personal growth, the sensation of being trapped or unable to move forward can be incredibly frustrating. However, developing a durable mind requires not just pushing through these moments but cultivating the mental flexibility to approach them in new ways. As discussed in the previous chapter, our expectations can serve as quicksand to our forward movement because the internal dialogue creates mental blocks. Inspired by the story "Stuck" by Oliver Jeffers, we can learn how we can build a more flexible and durable mind when faced with challenges that leave us feeling stuck.

Book Summary

It all started when Floyd's kite got caught in a tree… but things took a turn for the worse when he tried to free it by tossing a shoe, which also got stuck. Soon, he was hurling everything in sight—a ladder, a bucket of paint, even the kitchen sink, followed by an orangutan and, eventually, a whale who happened to be in the wrong place at the wrong time. And that was only the beginning. If only Floyd could produce a solution to fix it all once and for all. This is a hilarious tale of persistence and creativity from author Oliver Jeffers.

Understanding "Stuckness" – The Role of Limiting Beliefs

In "Stuck," the main character, Floyd, faces a seemingly simple problem—his kite gets stuck in a tree. However, instead of solving the problem with a clear approach, Floyd's thinking becomes more rigid, leading him to throw increasingly bizarre objects at the tree in a futile effort to free his kite. Floyd becomes attached to his approach, even though it is clear that it is not effective. His frustration grows as he continues to throw more objects into the tree, hoping for a different result. This is a common trap we fall into—thinking that if we just try harder, the same strategy will eventually work. This humorous yet insightful story reminds us of how we often approach problems: rather than stepping back and considering a new perspective, we double down on ineffective strategies, becoming even more stuck.

Like Floyd, our limiting beliefs—rigid ideas we hold about ourselves and our situations—often keep us stuck. These beliefs tell us that we cannot change, that things are just the way they are, that there are no other solutions or that we are not capable of finding them. To develop a durable mind, we need to recognize and challenge these limiting beliefs, embracing mental flexibility that allows us to find innovative approaches to old problems and to be willing to consider that previously used methods may not be effective with unfamiliar problems. Just because a way of approaching a problem seems familiar does not mean we should use solutions that are typical. Our rigidity has a close relationship to our desire for the safety that convenience and comfort tend to offer. The unknown presents variables that do not always fit neatly into our formulas for success. Being open to new ways can be risky as we negotiate narratives in our heads and from others that feed our fears instead of fanning our courage. This is why we need mental flexibility as a resource for progress.

A limiting perspective can multiply our rigid beliefs. When we feel stuck, our perspective often narrows, making it difficult to see alternative solutions or opportunities. Without a mindful approach we can end up with the misapplication of our determination to use the same strategy over and over again, preventing us from seeing other options and finding more effective solutions. Sometimes we do not need just another point of view, but more importantly we need to step back and reassess situations from a different viewing point! A durable mind requires the ability to zoom out and look at the bigger picture, rather than getting caught in the immediate frustration of being stuck. By shifting our viewing point, we can open ourselves to new possibilities and gain clarity on how to move forward.

This transition involves stepping back from viewing the world through a narrow lens shaped by personal experiences, biases, and assumptions, to intentionally observing the bigger picture. To make this shift, we must first examine what is influencing how we see the situation. Next, we need the courage to investigate whether our perspective is incomplete or if other valid views exist. This process challenges us to ask, *"What am I missing?"* and to shift from thinking, *"This is happening to me,"* to *"This is happening for me—what can I learn?"*

An important strategy in helping us get new viewing points is recognizing, engaging, and utilizing the power of other voices from a variety of sources including those that are familiar and those that are not. In *"Stuck,"* Floyd's struggle is largely solitary—he is determined to solve the problem on his own. However, in our own lives, we often need the input and guidance of others to help us see solutions we might have missed. Sometimes, the most valuable thing we can do when we feel stuck is to reach out for support. A durable mind recognizes that asking for help is not a sign of weakness but a step toward growth. By allowing others to provide new perspectives, suggestions, or advice, we can broaden and break free from the limitations of our own thinking.

Expanding your view is a gift—it allows you to see what was previously hidden because you were too close to the situation. Imagine looking through a keyhole and then stepping back to view the world through a wide window. The viewing point reveals greater context, colors, and connections that the keyhole couldn't capture. It invites exploration and discovery rather than assumptions and limitations.

This mindset shift—moving from a point of view to a viewing point—doesn't mean abandoning your perspective. Instead, it strengthens your ability to engage with complexity, adapt to change, and respond to challenges with resilience and insight.

Letting Go – The Key to a Durable Mind

In "Stuck," Floyd's problem is not just the kite in the tree—it is also his inability to see beyond his initial approach. It is hard to accept another perspective if our minds are not flexible enough to consider and value other options. Letting go is the ability to adapt your thinking and approach when faced with obstacles or challenges. A durable mind is not one that never faces difficulties but one that can find creative solutions when difficulties arise.

To cultivate a durable mind, we must learn to recognize when our strategies are not working and be willing to pivot. Learning to let go of our rigid way of thinking is a critical component of developing a durable mind because it enables us to shift our focus from what is not working to what might work instead. It teaches us to be open to new possibilities and creative solutions, which are essential when we feel stuck. This pliability allows us to look at problems from different angles, seek new information, and remain open to alternative solutions. It is not about avoiding problems but about building the capacity to respond to them in ways that promote growth and resilience.

Reframing Rigidity: Shifting from Fixed to Flexible Thinking

Rigid thinking often stems from a desire for control. Like Floyd in *Stuck*, we may find ourselves doubling down on methods that aren't working because we're too fixated on one outcome. Floyd's decision to throw increasingly absurd objects at the tree is a humorous yet cautionary tale about the dangers of sticking to ineffective strategies.

This same rigidity shows up in our lives when we resist change, cling to specific outcomes, or fear trying something new. However, flexibility begins with a shift in perspective. Mental flexibility is the ability to reframe setbacks as opportunities, explore creative solutions, and remain open to new approaches. Instead of getting stuck in frustration, we ask ourselves:

- *What else could this mean?*
- *What other options are available?*
- *Is there another way to approach this problem?*

When we develop this mental agility, we build a durable mind that allows us to thrive, even when life doesn't go according to plan.

The Bamboo and the Oak: A Story of Strength Through Flexibility

Once, in a dense forest, there stood a mighty oak tree and a small bamboo grove. The oak prided itself on its strength, believing its rigid trunk could withstand any storm. One day, a powerful wind swept through the forest. The bamboo bent and swayed with the gusts, adapting to the force of the storm, while the oak resisted and eventually snapped. The next morning, the bamboo stood tall, untouched, while the oak lay broken on the forest floor—*author unknown*

The lesson is clear: rigidity may appear strong, but true durability comes from being flexible in the face of adversity.

This parable parallels Floyd's experience in *Stuck.* His rigidity, like the oak's, prevents him from solving his problem effectively. Only when we learn to "bend" mentally—adapting to circumstances and trying new approaches—can we overcome life's storms which often require us to bend, not break. When we are willing to adapt, shift, and grow, we build the durability needed to overcome even the fiercest challenges.

Having adaptability is also about embracing change and uncertainty. In *"Stuck,"* Floyd's resistance to trying something new keeps him trapped in a cycle of failure. Similarly, in our own lives, resisting change and clinging to certainty can prevent us from making progress. A durable mind is one that is willing to face uncertainty with confidence, knowing that change is not something to fear but something to embrace. Letting go of what no longer works is one of the most challenging steps in moving forward. Often, we cling to old habits, thought patterns, or approaches out of familiarity, even when they no longer serve us. While letting go can feel like a defeat, it is actually a crucial step toward growth. Fear of the unknown often keeps people stuck in familiar but unproductive patterns. It means we must learn to tolerate discomfort and uncertainty, understanding that flexibility and adaptability are key to long-term resilience. A durable mind is one that understands when to persist and when to pivot, recognizing that this balance is essential for overcoming obstacles and making progress.

The Power of Action in Overcoming "Stuckness"

However, getting unstuck is not just about the ability to change your thinking, it also requires action. In *"Stuck,"* Floyd's determination to free his kite is commendable, even if his methods are misguided. His persistence teaches us that taking action, even without a perfect plan, is better than remaining trapped in inaction. Action, flawed as it may be, propels us forward and breaks the cycle of feeling stuck. The longer we stay stuck, the harder it becomes to regain the momentum needed for progress and the more prone we are to overthinking. Even small steps forward can rebuild confidence and generate the momentum required to overcome obstacles. A durable mind does not wait for perfect conditions, it remains proactive and continues moving forward, even when uncertainty clouds the path ahead.

Strategies For Developing Mental Flexibility

1. Meditation trains the mind to pause before reacting or responding to a situation. It increases self-awareness by allowing for reflection of thoughts and emotions that may be contributing to rigid patterns. Setting aside time to engage in meditation can lower stress and anxiety assisting with a willingness to consider other viewpoints.

2. Games & Puzzles are excellent tools for enhancing mental flexibility because they:

    - Require planning, predicting, and adapting to an opponent's moves which strengthens your ability to think ahead, shift strategies, and remain flexible in response to unexpected changes.

    - Train your brain to recognize patterns and think creatively.

    - Often require making quick decisions, weighing risks and rewards, and sometimes dealing with imperfect information.

    - Challenge you to try different approaches and keep going even after failed attempts, teaching you not to stick rigidly to a single method and helping you to explore and adapt when needed.

   - Improve working memory and focus which is essential for holding and processing multiple ideas at once, simultaneously allowing you to move between different ideas or perspectives more easily.
   - Strengthen your mental agility, allowing you to approach challenges with a more open, adaptable mindset and a readiness to try new solutions.

3. Relentless learning is taking the time to learn small chunks of information from different areas, both relevant and non-relevant to your life. It strengthens a durable mind by enhancing adaptability, building resilience, and fostering a growth-oriented approach to life's challenges. By making continuous learning a habit, we equip ourselves with the skills, confidence, and perspective needed to face adversity with determination and resilience.

Conclusion

Developing a durable mind means learning to move beyond frustration and rigid thinking, embracing flexibility in both thought and action. When we feel stuck, it is easy to focus on what is not working and double down on the same ineffective strategies. However, true progress requires us to pause, shift perspectives, and explore new possibilities. Instead of fixating on a single solution, we can ask ourselves, *"What other options are available?"* or *"What resources have I yet to explore?"* These questions invite curiosity and innovation, two essential components of mental durability.

Floyd's story in *Stuck* serves as a humorous but powerful reminder that persistence alone is not enough; we must also be willing to adapt. The ability to step back, reassess, and pivot when needed is what ultimately allows us to break free from stagnation. A durable mind is not one that avoids challenges but one that actively engages with them, knowing that forward movement—no matter how small—is better than standing still.

While feeling stuck is a common experience, it does not have to define us or our progress. By cultivating mental flexibility and practicing resilience, we unlock the ability to navigate uncertainty with confidence. Whether in our personal endeavors or leadership roles, learning to shift perspectives, adjust to new circumstances, and welcome change empowers us to overcome obstacles and continue growing. The key to getting unstuck is not waiting for the perfect solution but developing the adaptability to create momentum, one step at a time.

🎙 *For more insights and personal stories related to this chapter, listen to Episode 4 of The Life Sculptors Podcast:*

- **Episode Title:** "How To Get Unstuck."
- **Listen Here:** https://youtu.be/B8vI5Mixs5A

Durability Lab: Cultivating Mental Flexibility Through Thought Reframing

Developing mental flexibility takes practice. Here's an exercise to help you start reframing your thinking:

- **Identify a Stuck Thought**: Write down a recurring negative thought (e.g., *"I'm not good at this, so I shouldn't try."*).
- **Reframe It**: Ask yourself:
    - *Is this thought completely true?*
    - *What evidence contradicts this thought?*
    - *What is a more empowering way to view this situation?*
      For example: *"I'm not good at this, yet. I can improve by practicing and learning."*
- **Take Action**: Write down one small step you can take to move forward with a new mindset.

The next time you catch yourself stuck in rigid thinking, pause and ask, "What's another way I can approach this situation?" Practice this often to build the mental agility that helps you adapt and grow.

Chapter 7 Durability Reflection Questions

As you reflect on this chapter, consider where you might be feeling stuck in your own life. Remember, a durable mind is one that is open to change, flexible in its thinking, and committed to taking action, even when the path is not clear.

- When you feel stuck, how can you shift your focus from frustration to curiosity? What questions can you ask yourself to explore new perspectives?
- How often do you explore multiple solutions to a problem rather than fixating on a single answer? What might you gain by broadening your approach?

- What recent challenge allowed you to demonstrate resilience? How did this experience contribute to your growth and adaptability?
- How comfortable are you with adding "yet" to areas where you feel limited? What is one area where this mindset could open up new possibilities?
- What daily practices can you adopt to strengthen your mental flexibility? How can these practices prepare you to handle uncertainty with confidence?

NOTES

CHAPTER 8: PERSISTENCE AND ADAPTABILITY

"Do not judge me by my successes, judge me by how many times I fell down and got back up again." -Nelson Mandela

Introduction

Persistence and determination are vital qualities for developing a durable mind. They are the driving forces that keep us moving forward, even when obstacles arise, or progress feels slow. Combined with the power of dreams, they help us maintain hope, an essential element in building mental resilience. In this chapter, inspired by the book "A Frog Thing" by Eric Drachrum, we explore what persistence and determination really mean, how they are developed, and how dreams fuel the hope that sustains us through life's challenges.

Book Summary

A Frog Thing tells the story of Frank, a young frog with a big dream—he wants to fly like the birds he sees soaring through the sky. Despite being told repeatedly by his family and other frogs that frogs cannot fly, Frank remains determined to achieve his goal. He tries many ways to take flight, but none of his attempts are successful. Eventually, Frank meets a friendly bird who understands his desire to fly. The bird offers to take Frank for a ride, allowing him to experience flight in a way he never expected. Through this experience, Frank learns that even though he cannot fly on his own, he can still find creative ways to achieve his dreams. The story is a heartwarming tale about determination, persistence, and the importance of being creative to reach your goals. It teaches readers that even if their dreams seem impossible, there may be alternative ways to fulfill them.

What Is Persistence?

Persistence is the ability to continue working toward a goal, despite encountering setbacks or difficulties. It is about holding onto a vision and pushing forward, even when the path is not clear, or the outcome is not guaranteed. In *"A Frog Thing,"* Frank's persistence is evident in his determination to fly, even though he is told repeatedly that frogs cannot fly. Rather than accepting this limitation, Frank continues to pursue his dream, trying different methods and refusing to give up.

Persistence does not mean ignoring reality or recklessly pursuing a goal without adjusting to challenges. Instead, it is about having mental stamina to keep trying, learning from failures, and adapting along the way. In this way, persistence becomes a cornerstone of mental resilience. It teaches us that setbacks are not final; they are part of the journey to success.

Developing Persistence and Determination

Persistence and determination are not traits we are born with; they are developed over time, through experience and practice. One of the most effective ways to cultivate persistence is by setting small, manageable goals and working consistently toward them. Each small success reinforces our belief in our ability to achieve larger goals, and each failure teaches us how to improve.

In *"A Frog Thing,"* Frank's persistence is fueled by his determination to achieve something that seems impossible. His dream of flying is what keeps him going, despite the repeated setbacks. Similarly, determination is the inner drive that propels us forward when we want to give up. It is the force that helps us push through moments of doubt, frustration, or fatigue.

Building determination involves cultivating a mindset that welcomes challenges as opportunities for growth. This requires us to reframe failures not as roadblocks but as steppingstones. Every time Frank tries and fails and tries again, he builds his capacity to persist. His determination grows stronger because he learns that while the path to success may not be linear, it is possible if he keeps pushing forward. Building a durable mind means understanding that persistence is not just about immediate success—it is about being willing to try, fail, learn, and try again.

The Role of Dreams in Developing Persistence

At some point, everyone has at least one big dream. It lingers in our minds, gnaws at our souls, and seeks manifestation. Dreams inspire us to believe beyond our current conditions, pushing us toward possibilities that might seem out of reach.

Frank's parents told him, "***You can do whatever you set your mind to.***" How many of us have heard this expression from parents, teachers, or mentors? It's a message meant to inspire confidence and determination, but it raises an important question:

Is it really true? Can we do whatever we set our minds to?

If this statement is taken literally, does that mean those who didn't achieve their dreams simply didn't work hard enough? Have generations of parents and educators been untruthful, offering false hope?

This question creates *cognitive dissonance*, the psychological discomfort that arises when we hold two conflicting beliefs at the same time. (Festinger) On the one hand, we are taught to believe that hard work and determination can lead to any outcome we desire. On the other hand, reality teaches us that effort alone does not always guarantee success. This internal tension forces us to rethink our assumptions, adjust our approach, and find new ways to persist despite uncertainty. History is full of examples of individuals who defied the odds, achieved what others believed couldn't be done, and shattered barriers in the process. But we also know that not everyone who dreams of being an astronaut, an Olympic athlete, or a world-renowned artist will necessarily achieve that exact vision. So how do we reconcile these two realities?

The truth is, we may not be able to do *everything*, but we can always do *something.* Dreams should not be dismissed simply because they seem beyond our reach. Instead, they should serve as motivation to push us further, to help us explore what *is* possible, and to encourage persistence in the face of obstacles.

Rather than focusing on whether *everything* is achievable, the more empowering questions are:

- What steps can I take toward my dream?
- How can I adapt when challenges arise?
- What is within my control that can move me forward?

Dreams, when paired with persistence, do not just offer hope—they cultivate resilience. They remind us that even if we cannot accomplish *everything*, we can take meaningful steps forward. And sometimes, taking those steps is what truly transforms us. In this way, dreams become more than just aspirations; they act as anchors of hope, guiding us through roads filled with uncertainty and adversity all the while, providing direction and purpose.

The Role of Dreams in Maintaining Hope

By their very nature, dreams give us something to reach for—an image of what could be, rather than what is. They sustain hope by offering a vision of the future that motivates us to keep moving forward, even when the present feels challenging. In *"A Frog Thing,"* Frank's dream of flying keeps him hopeful, even when his efforts do not immediately succeed. His dream provides him with the mental resilience to keep trying new things, even when others doubt him.

Dreams act as beacons of hope, guiding us through tough times and reminding us that the future holds possibilities we may not yet see. They help us focus on the long-term vision, rather than getting caught up in temporary failures. This sense of hope is crucial for maintaining a durable mind because it keeps us moving forward, even when the outcome is unclear.

However, dreams also need to be flexible. Frank's dream of flying does not come to fruition in the way he initially imagined, but through his persistence, he finds a creative solution. He learns to experience flight by riding on a stick held between the feet of two birds, which fulfills his dream in an unusual way. This moment highlights the importance of innovation which is a byproduct of developing a durable mind. When we face challenges, we can either become fixated on what we cannot do, or we can start thinking outside the box. The greater our cognitive plasticity, the more likely we are to be adaptable, constantly looking for new ways to overcome obstacles and make progress. This flexibility is important because it allows us to adapt our dreams to the realities we encounter, without losing hope or determination.

How Dreams Fuel Resilience

Dreams are not just about achieving a specific goal; they also play a vital role in building resilience. When we hold onto a dream, we are more likely to push through difficulties because we believe in the possibility of a better future. This belief fuels resilience, giving us the strength to keep going when things get tough.

Having a long-term bigger vision helps to sustain hope. Dreams provide that vision, allowing us to focus on something larger than the immediate challenges we face. When we are anchored by a dream, setbacks do not feel as devastating because we know they are temporary. The dream acts as a lifeline, pulling us through difficult moments and reminding us that perseverance will lead to success. It is important to stay committed to the bigger vision while being open to different paths toward achieving it.

The Role of Support in Building Resilience

Frank's journey is also supported by the creatures around him, including the birds that help him achieve flight. This highlights the importance of seeking support from others when pursuing our dreams. While resilience often feels like a solitary endeavor, building a durable mind is also about recognizing when to ask for help and allowing others to contribute to our journey.

Surrounding ourselves with supportive people can boost our mental resilience. It is not in our best interest to pursue our dreams in isolation because we find strength in community. By leaning on others when needed, we build emotional and mental support systems that help us persist through challenges.

The Intersection of Dreams, Persistence, and Determination

Persistence, determination, and dreams are all interconnected. Our dreams give us the motivation to pursue our goals, while persistence and determination provide the tools to overcome obstacles along the way. Together, they form the foundation of a durable mind.

Frank's story in *"A Frog Thing"* demonstrates this beautifully. His dream of flying gives him hope, while his determination pushes him to keep trying, and his persistence allows him to continue experimenting until he finds a solution. These qualities do not just help Frank achieve his goal; they also build his resilience and mental strength, preparing him for future challenges.

Conclusion

Frank's journey in *A Frog Thing* illustrates the powerful combination of dreams, persistence, and determination in building a durable mind. His unwavering dream of flying fuels his hope, while his persistence and determination guide him through setbacks, leading him to a creative solution. This story teaches us that resilience is not just about achieving our dreams in the exact way we imagine but about remaining open to alternative paths and finding strength in the process. By embracing our dreams, nurturing determination, and persisting even when the road is difficult, we build the mental resilience to face life's challenges. A durable mind is not deterred by obstacles—it adapts, evolves, and continues to strive toward a vision of possibility.

Persistence and determination are essential components of developing a durable mind. They give us the strength to keep going, even when the road is difficult, and help us learn from setbacks rather than being defeated by them. Dreams, on the other hand, fuel our hope and provide the motivation to push through tough times. Together, they create a powerful combination that helps us not only achieve our goals but also build the mental resilience to face future challenges.

For more insights and personal stories related to this chapter, listen to Episode 5 of The Life Sculptors Podcast:

- **Episode Title:** "Learning to Live Between the Now, Not Yet & Not Possible."
- **Listen Here:** https://youtu.be/3Wy3g55AYk4

Durability Lab: Strategies for Developing Persistence and Determination

1. **Reframe Failures as Steppingstones**

   Failures are not the end of the road; they are lessons in disguise. Frank's repeated attempts to fly, though unsuccessful at first, taught him resilience and creativity. Instead of viewing setbacks as barriers, see them as opportunities to grow.

2. **Practice Visualization**

   Take a moment to visualize your dream. Picture yourself achieving it—what does it look like, feel like, and mean to you? This mental exercise can keep you motivated and focused on your goals, even during difficult times.

3. **Set Incremental Goals**

   Break your larger dream into smaller, manageable steps. Achieving these smaller milestones reinforces your belief in your ability to reach the larger goal. For instance, if your dream is to write a book, start with a chapter outline or a daily word count goal.

For additional assistance with this lab, see the attached worksheet or click the link for a digital copy.

Reader Exercise: Persistence Journal

Create a persistence journal to track your progress toward a goal. Include sections for:

- **Setbacks:** Note the challenges you encounter and how they make you feel.
- **Lessons Learned:** Write down what each setback teaches you.
- **Steps Forward:** List actionable steps to move past the setback.
- **Successes:** Celebrate small wins along the way.

This exercise builds awareness of your persistence journey and reinforces your determination.

Chapter 8 Durability Reflection Questions

As you reflect on this chapter, consider the role that persistence, determination, and dreams have played in your own life. Remember, the journey toward your dreams may not always be easy, but with persistence, determination, and hope, you can build the strength needed to achieve them.

- What dream are you currently pursuing, and how does it provide you with hope and motivation? How might this dream keep you moving forward through setbacks?

- Think of a recent challenge where persistence and determination helped you overcome an obstacle. How did staying focused on your goal, despite difficulties, build your resilience?
- In what ways can you practice flexibility in pursuing your dreams? How might being open to unusual ways of achieving your goals support your mental resilience?
- How has the support of others helped you stay committed to your goals? What role does community play in helping you build a durable mind?
- Are there any areas in your life where you struggle with persistence or determination? What small steps could you take to strengthen these qualities and build resilience?

NOTES

DURABILITY LAB MILESTONE #4

Embracing Adaptability Through Challenge & Growth

Adaptability is a fundamental trait of a durable mind, allowing us to pivot, adjust, and navigate uncertainty with confidence. Challenges will always arise, but our ability to adapt determines whether we stay stuck or move forward.

Chapters 7 & 8 highlight the importance of mental flexibility—learning to shift perspectives, reframe obstacles, and take action, even in the face of uncertainty. Floyd in *Stuck* doubled down on the same ineffective strategy, while Frank in *A Frog Thing* demonstrated persistence in the pursuit of his dream. These stories remind us that true adaptability is about learning, adjusting, and evolving rather than remaining rigid in our approach.

This milestone will help you track your progress in becoming more adaptable by recognizing growth, overcoming challenges, and reinforcing lessons learned.

The Growth Jar (Interactive Visual Aid)

Adaptability is built through reflection and reinforcement. Use this activity to acknowledge your progress.

🔑 **Marker:** Keep a Growth Jar and add at least one note per week acknowledging:

- A situation where you adapted to a challenge.
- A lesson learned from shifting your approach.
- A breakthrough moment when you overcame a mental block.

Over time, you will see tangible evidence of your adaptability growing.

Challenge Log

Challenges often feel like roadblocks but documenting how you adapt to them strengthens resilience and creates a personal blueprint for problem-solving.

🔍 **Marker:** Maintain a Challenge Log to:

- Record obstacles you've faced.
- Reflect on how you adapted and adjusted.
- Identify strategies that worked (or didn't) and why.

Revisit this log whenever you feel stuck to remind yourself that you have the capacity to overcome obstacles and grow through change.

Final Thought

Adaptability is not about avoiding difficulties—it's about learning how to navigate them effectively. The more you practice shifting perspectives, adjusting strategies, and embracing uncertainty, the more you strengthen your ability to stay durable and flexible in the face of life's challenges. Keep pushing forward, keep learning, and keep growing into a more adaptable version of yourself!

KEY #5: MOTIVATION

Internal Drive For Growth

Motivation is the driving force that keeps us moving forward, even when challenges arise. It is the internal spark that propels us toward growth, resilience, and meaningful action. A durable mind is not just about enduring hardship, it is about cultivating the drive to push through obstacles with intention and purpose.

In Chapters 9 and 10, we explore how motivation is shaped by both internal and external factors, and how we can harness it to sustain long-term growth. Chapter 9 delves into the emotional defenses we use to shield ourselves from vulnerability, while Chapter 10 explores the hunger that fuels our desires and the balance needed to manage them effectively. Both chapters highlight the importance of self-awareness in maintaining motivation, understanding what truly drives us and ensuring our efforts align with our values and well-being.

Developing a durable mind requires not only persistence but also the wisdom to assess whether our motivations are serving us or leading us toward exhaustion and emotional depletion. The Durability Lab Milestone for this section will help you reflect on your motivations, refine your goals, and develop strategies to sustain your drive in a way that fosters long-term resilience.

CHAPTER 9: THE ARMOR OF APPEARANCE AND ATTITUDE

"Vulnerability is not winning or losing; it's having the courage to show up and be seen when we have no control over the outcome."
— Brené Brown

Introduction

Imagine a tightly closed fist. It seems strong and unyielding, yet it cannot hold anything new. Now, picture an open hand. Though it may appear vulnerable, it can receive, hold, and give. This metaphor captures the paradox of vulnerability: defensiveness may feel like protection, but true strength lies in openness and connection. Vulnerability, far from being a weakness, serves as a wellspring of resilience and growth, allowing us to expand beyond our emotional armor.

When we feel vulnerable, it's common to build defenses—whether through appearance, attitude, or behavior—to shield ourselves from pain. These defenses may offer temporary protection, but over time, they isolate us from meaningful connections and limit our emotional growth. In Buffalo Fluffalo by Bess Kalb, the main character uses both his fluffy appearance and a defensive attitude to shield himself from the judgment and rejection of others. This chapter explores how relying on perceived strength and emotional armor impacts the development of a durable mind, and how embracing vulnerability fosters true resilience and deeper connections.

Book Summary

The story of Buffalo Fluffalo, a grumpy and fluffy buffalo that rejects the friendship offers of the friendly creatures in his neighborhood is told in Bess Kalb's picture book BUFFALO FLUFFALO (Random House Studio, 2024) and drawn by Erin Kraan. But after a rainstorm causes Fluffalo to lose his fluff and turns him into a drippy mess, he learns to accept comfort from others. BUFFALO FLUFFALO is a tender story about friendship and feelings.

Appearance as a Defense

In *Buffalo Fluffalo*, the protagonist's fluffy appearance sets him apart from the other animals, and rather than embracing his uniqueness, he uses it as a shield to keep others at a distance. His fluffy coat becomes a physical barrier that he hides behind, hoping it will protect him from being judged or hurt by others. By relying on his appearance as armor, Fluffalo insulates himself from vulnerability, but in doing so, he also isolates himself from the support and acceptance he truly desires, but there is a difference between isolation and insulation. To insulate is to wrap something or someone with something that protects against loss by limiting access, preventing unwanted connection, interaction, or intrusions. We are familiar with insulation in our homes that serves to slow the spread of heat, noise or cold.

Sometimes people insulate by using aspects of their appearance such as weight, muscles, make-up, clothing styles, etc. to protect themselves emotionally. Whether it is dressing or acting a certain way to avoid attention or to appear tougher, these choices can create an illusion of control over how we are perceived. Using appearance as emotional armor may protect us in the short term, but it limits the way we were designed to live, thriving in community.

Post-Pandemic Social Isolation and Resilience

The COVID-19 pandemic profoundly reshaped the ways we experience connection and resilience. Social isolation, while necessary for public health, disrupted interpersonal relationships and increased feelings of loneliness. These shifts have lasting implications for how we process vulnerability and build durable minds.

Isolation during the pandemic led many to rely more heavily on emotional defenses, such as presenting a tough exterior or retreating entirely from social interactions. The absence of regular, meaningful connections created a breeding ground for fear and insecurity, as individuals grappled with uncertainty and loss. This mirrors Fluffalo's journey, where his defenses isolate him from the very support he needs.

However, the pandemic also highlighted the importance of fostering emotional resilience. Studies have shown that practices such as mindfulness, journaling, and cultivating vulnerability can help mitigate the psychological effects of isolation. (vtzan) These strategies are essential for transitioning from isolation to reconnection, underscoring the need for a durable mind that balances self-protection with openness.

The lessons of post-pandemic resilience remind us that true strength lies in our ability to adapt, embrace vulnerability, and rebuild meaningful relationships. Fluffalo's transformation from isolation to connection serves as a microcosm of this broader societal journey.

Attitude as a Shield

Beyond appearance, Fluffalo also adopts a defensive attitude to shield himself from emotional pain. His outward demeanor becomes an additional layer of protection, projecting a sense of indifference or toughness to discourage others from seeing his true feelings. This defensive attitude is common when we feel vulnerable, as we try to mask our insecurities with a facade of confidence or aloofness. However, this attitude often deepens our sense of isolation.

We have all come across or interacted with someone who just seems "mean," abrasive, or hard to connect with because they do not seem to let anyone get close. They use their attitude as a way to protect themselves from hurt and have even told everyone else and themselves that they do not care what other people think or feel. This apathetic approach can include putting up emotional walls, acting indifferent to criticism, or presenting an overly tough exterior. These attitudes can block genuine connection because they appear on the surface to be a healthy boundary. Creating a boundary is important but it must be done thoughtfully requiring responsiveness and not reactivity. When we are reactive, we can tend to apply the wrong strategy to situations causing further harm to ourselves and others. A durable mind recognizes that while these defenses may provide temporary safety, they also prevent us from being open to the emotional risks necessary for growth and resilience. By clinging to a defensive attitude, we avoid the vulnerability that allows us to experience meaningful relationships and personal development.

The Emotional Cost of Isolating Ourselves

While using appearance and attitude as armor may help protect us from immediate hurt, it comes with emotional costs. When our efforts to insulate are not successful and we do not deal with the offenses that led to this kind of fortress building, they result in isolation. In *Buffalo Fluffalo*, Fluffalo's decision to use his fluffy appearance and defensive attitude to shield himself leads to feelings of isolation. He is unable to connect with others on a deeper level, and his fear of being judged or rejected keeps him emotionally distant from those around him. His primary emotion of choice is anger. Anger is useful but it is not intended to be your permanent state. The volume of your angst is an indication of the depth of your hurt, not the girth of your strength.

Sometimes our use of anger to insulate is really about the shame we feel because of what has happened to us. Our shame will have us feeling like we are unworthy of love, attention, help, relationships, or support. Isolation is an unhealthy attempt at erecting a boundary and is applied when we have experienced "unsafe" situations in our relationships. While creating boundaries is a necessary skill for relationships, the type of boundary we build will determine if we are cutting off an important life source…people. We need relationships like we need food, water, air, and blood. Here are some signs that you may be isolating:

- Being overly confrontational
- Cutting off emotionally or physically
- Feeling alone despite having relationships with others
- Thinking no one understands you
- Avoiding close relationships due to fear of getting hurt
- Keeping people at a distance because you do not trust them
- Going through lengthy periods of not interacting with others

These are just some indicators that you may have built a fortress around yourself and are on the pathway to isolation.

The Role of Fear in Emotional Defenses

At the core of both our reliance on appearance and our defensive attitude is fear; fear of being judged, fear of rejection, and fear of not being accepted. Our attitude and tough demeanor give us a sense of control over how others perceive us, but they also reinforce our underlying fears by preventing us from experiencing true acceptance. While these defenses may help us feel safer in the moment, they also reinforce the very fears we are trying to avoid. A durable mind confronts fear by embracing vulnerability rather than avoiding it. By acknowledging our fears and working through them, we become more resilient and less dependent on external defenses.

Moving Beyond Appearance and Attitude as Armor

The path to building a durable mind involves moving beyond the need to use appearance and attitude as armor. In *Buffalo Fluffalo*, Fluffalo's journey toward self-acceptance marks a turning point in his emotional growth. When he begins to let go of his need to hide behind his fluffy appearance and defensive attitude, he discovers that his uniqueness is something to be embraced, not hidden. This transformation allows him to connect more appropriately through insulation and more deeply with others to build a stronger sense of self-worth. The right kind of boundaries help us insulate appropriately. We cannot always create the geographical distance we want from some people (i.e., we work with them, or they are family, or they are our neighbors) but we can learn to insulate by thinking our way through situations instead of feeling our way through. And sometimes the enormity of what we have gone through or the duration we have been in a situation causes us to become mired in our feelings, thinking, and behavior.

Insulation requires reflection. When you have been wounded and you have not dealt well with it, you will resist attempts at intimacy or connection and life has a way of exposing what you refuse to deal with or let go of. It is imperative that we stop perpetuating unhelpful and unhealthy mental, emotional, and relational habits because they subtly undermine our effectiveness and efforts to have peace. True resilience comes from letting down emotional defenses and embracing vulnerability. Moving beyond the need to protect ourselves with appearance or attitude means allowing others to see us as we truly are. While this openness may expose us to hurt, it also opens the door to deeper connections and personal growth. A durable mind learns to balance vulnerability with resilience, knowing that the strength to face life's challenges comes from within, not from external defenses.

Conclusion

Fluffalo's journey teaches us that true resilience comes not from hiding behind external defenses, but from embracing vulnerability and authenticity. By letting go of the need to shield ourselves with appearance or attitude, we allow ourselves to face the emotional risks that lead to real growth and connection. Vulnerability may expose us to pain, but it also opens the door to deeper relationships and a stronger sense of self-worth. Embracing who he is, Fluffalo learns that his value is not determined by his appearance or how tough he seems, but by his willingness to be authentic.

A durable mind recognizes that strength is found not in the walls we build around us, but in our willingness to be seen as we are, flaws and all. Through this openness, we build a mind capable of facing life's challenges with resilience, courage, and a genuine connection to others.

For more insights and personal stories related to this chapter, listen to Episode 10 of The Life Sculptors Podcast:

- **Episode Title:** "Enough Is Enough. Stop Isolating. Start Insulating."
- **Listen Here:** https://youtu.be/p58oSKpIznM

 Durability Lab: Harnessing Motivation Through Reframing Failure

Durability Lab:

Failure can either be a roadblock or a redirection—it all depends on how we interpret it. A durable mind does not view failure as an endpoint, but rather as a turning point for growth and self-discovery. Motivation thrives when we shift our perspective, learn from setbacks, and continue moving forward with renewed purpose. The exercises in this lab will help you reframe failure, regulate emotions, and use setbacks as steppingstones toward resilience.

1. **Change the Narrative**

Failures are not conclusions; they are chapters in your ongoing story. Instead of saying, *"I failed,"* try shifting your language to *"This attempt didn't work out, but here's what I learned."* By reframing the experience, you move from a mindset of defeat to one of growth. Every misstep provides valuable insights that refine your approach and strengthen your resolve.

2. 2. Embrace Emotional Granularity

When faced with setbacks, broad labels like "frustrated" or "upset" can limit our ability to process emotions effectively. As Dr. Lisa Feldman Barrett explains, emotional granularity is the skill of identifying and differentiating between emotions with precision. Are you feeling discouraged, embarrassed, or uncertain? The more accurately you name your emotions, the better you can understand and manage them.

To assist with identifying and naming emotions, consider using a **Feelings Wheel** (feelingswheel.com). This tool expands your emotional vocabulary, helping you explore what you're truly experiencing. Strengthening emotional awareness empowers you to respond intentionally rather than react impulsively, keeping motivation intact even in the face of challenges.

3. 3. Reframe Setbacks as Redirections

When obstacles arise, instead of asking *"Why is this happening to me?"* consider asking *"What new path is opening up?"* Roadblocks often force us to explore alternative solutions, uncover hidden strengths, or pursue opportunities we would not have otherwise considered. Motivation grows when we see setbacks not as dead ends, but as detours guiding us toward new possibilities.

Reader Exercise: The Failure Reframe Journal

Create a **Failure Reframe Journal** to document and analyze setbacks in a productive way. Use the following structure:

- **The Event:** Describe what happened in detail.
- **Initial Emotions:** Write down your immediate emotional response.

- **Lessons Learned:** Reflect on the insights this experience provided.
- **Next Steps:** Identify one concrete action you can take to move forward.
- **Silver Lining:** Highlight something positive that emerged from this setback.

Review your entries periodically to track your growth and see how your perspective shifts over time. As you build the habit of reframing failure, you will cultivate a mindset that fuels motivation rather than diminishes it.

Final Thought

Developing a durable mind means staying motivated even when things do not go as planned. Setbacks are inevitable, but with the right perspective, they become fuel for persistence, learning, and growth. By engaging in these exercises, you strengthen your ability to bounce back, adapt, and remain motivated on your journey toward personal and professional success.

Chapter 9 Durability Reflection Questions

As you reflect on this chapter, consider how appearance and attitude might play a role in your own emotional defenses. Remember, a durable mind is not one that avoids vulnerability, it is one that embraces it as a pathway to strength and authentic living.

- Are there aspects of your appearance or attitude that you use as a shield to protect yourself from emotional pain? How might letting go of these defenses open you up to deeper connections?
- Think about a time when you avoided vulnerability by isolating yourself. How did this impact your

relationships and emotional well-being? What would it look like to embrace vulnerability in similar situations?

- What fears might be driving you to rely on external defenses? How could confronting these fears and embracing vulnerability help you build resilience and a durable mind?
- How might creating thoughtful boundaries, rather than reactive defenses, help you feel safe while still allowing for meaningful relationships?

NOTES

Chapter 10: Managing Hunger and Drive

"You cannot fill a cup that is already full. Sometimes, you must empty yourself of what is holding you back to make room for something better." — Unknown

Introduction

At some point in our lives, we all face hunger—whether it is hunger for validation, connection, success, or even material security. How we manage that hunger shapes our resilience and mental durability. To be human is to have longings and loves. Our hearts are the place where they are incubated and the environments, we get exposed to create the conditions for our hungers to find expression. It is like we have been hardwired to be on the move, pursuing something. We live leaning forward, towards what we want…what our souls' hunger for, although at times we get stuck looking back. In *The Three Billy Goats Gruff*, retold by Mac Barnett, the troll's insatiable hunger leads him down a path of greed and isolation, ultimately blocking his growth. This chapter explores how unchecked desires can erode mental strength and how cultivating self-awareness, moderation, and connection helps us build a durable mind.

Book Summary

In this classic tale, three Billy goats attempt to cross a bridge to reach the lush grass on the other side. However, a fearsome troll lives under the bridge and threatens to eat anyone who tries to cross. When the three Billy Goats Gruff decide to clip-clop across the bridge to get to the grassy ridge, the troll is already imagining all the ways to prepare a delicious goat dinner. But the troll underestimates those seemingly sweet but oh-so-savvy goats! The three goats, each progressively bigger than the last, use cleverness and bravery to confront the troll. Through their determination, they eventually outwit the troll and safely make it across. Mac Barnett's retelling introduces a new narrative voice while retaining the timeless lesson at the heart of the story.

The Hunger for More – Balancing Need and Greed

In *The Three Billy Goats Gruff*, the troll guards the bridge with an insatiable hunger that goes beyond mere survival. His greed compels him to control access to the bridge, seeing every passerby as a resource to exploit and consume. This behavior illustrates the tension between need and greed; a conflict we all face when our desires spiral beyond what is necessary into something destructive. Unmanaged hunger, whether for success, validation, or control, can distort our thinking and priorities.

It is also possible to view the troll's greed as emotional armor, a means of protecting oneself from weakness and the fear of scarcity. Even while this armor can seem safe, in the end it separates him and prevents him from connecting or developing. As hard as it may seem, letting go of these protections enables us to develop closer bonds with others and discover the real power of transparency. A durable mind requires an ability to discern the difference between what is essential and what is driven by fear or insecurity. Greed stems from a deep emotional hunger that seeks more of something because of an internal sense of lack. But true durability comes from recognizing when our hunger is about more than just needs and learning to manage our desires before they take control. Let's explore what may be behind our hunger.

Desperation, Emotional Blind Spots, and Greed

Desperation is often the fuel that drives us toward greed. In *The Three Billy Goats Gruff*, the troll's desperation to control the bridge blinds him to the bigger picture and to the needs of others. His hunger, unchecked by self-awareness, isolates him, and limits his ability to grow or adapt. When our lives experience relational or connectional famine, we have a tough time seeing things through the lens of what others maybe experiencing of us because our desperation has clouded our judgment resulting in blind spots. When we are driven by unchecked hunger, whether it is for connection, recognition, or material gain, we lose sight of the impact our actions have on others and on ourselves. A durable mind recognizes desperation as a signal to pause and reflect, to reassess whether our pursuit is truly aligned with our values or if it is driven by fear or inadequacy. By addressing the emotional roots of desperation, we can cultivate the mental strength to act from a place of balance, rather than scarcity.

The troll's greed in *The Three Billy Goats Gruff* is more than just a desire for resources, it is a defense mechanism. By controlling the bridge and demanding more from each traveler, the troll insulates himself from vulnerability. Greed can become a tool we use to shield ourselves from the emotional starvation of loneliness and insecurity. In doing so, we cut off the possibility of meaningful connection or personal growth as others only see us as consumers or worst yet "users"—someone whose motivation is only what they can get from others.

Motivated by our instinct to protect, our greed frequently acts as emotional armor. This often manifests as selfishness, uncooperative behavior, or even bullying due to the aggressive nature that accompanies our desperation. At the heart of greed there is often a sense of shame that is deeply connected to an underlying belief that we are not enough as we are. This shame leads us to overcompensate by seeking more: more success, more validation, more power. In *The Three Billy Goats Gruff*, the troll's insatiable appetite reflects his deeper emotional hunger, a need to fill the emptiness caused by his isolation and lack of connection. A durable mind, however, sees through this illusion and understands that true strength does not come from hoarding or controlling resources, but from embracing vulnerability and connection. By breaking down these emotional defenses, we allow ourselves to grow, connect, and strengthen our resilience. When we accept vulnerability, we can discover true strength and are able to shed the armor that desperation and fear have conditioned us to wear. This transformation allows for more meaningful interactions and a better understanding of how to treat underlying emotional needs.

The Importance of Moderation in Developing Resilience

A key component of mental durability is moderation—knowing when to pursue a goal and when to step back. In *The Three Billy Goats Gruff*, the troll's lack of moderation leads to his downfall. The paradox of greed is that without moderation, our greed can blind us to the fact that taking more than is needed leads to having less. Unchecked ambition or hunger can lead to burnout, disconnection, and emotional depletion. Developing a durable mind through the practice of moderation comes from a place of understanding the importance of balance. It is not about rejecting ambition or desire but about managing longings and loves in a way that supports long-term growth and resilience. By practicing moderation, we create space for reflection, connection, and recovery which are key elements of a durable mind.

---

*"Hunger is not just about food—it is the driving force that makes us chase dreams, build empires, and transform our lives. But hunger without discipline leads to destruction." — **Lisa Nichols***

Connection as a Remedy for Hunger

One of the central elements in the life of the troll in *The Three Billy Goats Gruff* is that he operates alone. His greed in many ways has robbed him of a community to help him manage his desires so that his intentions are aligned with his behaviors. There is nothing wrong with our hunger and typically our intentions are not maligned by malice in our hearts. When we function in isolation, our famine sense of belonging causes misalignment of our behaviors as we act out of relational malnourishment. Without meaningful connections, the troll in us turns to domination and greed to fill the emotional void. Loneliness is a form of starvation, and connection is the nourishment we need to thrive.

One of the elements of our greedy defenses that serves as a barrier to meaningful connection is something called reaction formation, the mechanism by which we convert a feeling into its opposite. We idealize something so we do not feel negative emotions about it. In other words, we convince ourselves that our greed is just a high drive for success, and this is a valuable quality for successful people. And how do we measure what is too much? Dian Couto, a journalist and psychology editor with The Harvard Business Review, wrote "*it is society that decrees how much greed is enough—how we define where healthy ambition ends and unsavory self-interest begins.* " (Couto, 2003) We need a community to help us stay balanced in our desires for greed is not just about acquiring more for me, but it also is about withholding something from others.

A durable mind recognizes that fulfillment does not come from accumulating more but from building relationships and contributing to the well-being of others. Maybe generosity is another antidote to our greed as it shifts our focus from just living for ourselves to learning to live with and for each other. By fostering connection, we counter the feelings of inadequacy that drive greed and build a foundation of emotional resilience. True strength comes not from controlling others but from building a life of generosity, collaboration, and mutual support. When we let go of emotional armor, we allow ourselves to be seen and supported. This vulnerability is a sign of resilience rather than weakness. Our brains and hearts are nourished when we drop our barriers because it creates the intimacy and trust necessary for real connection.

Conclusion

The tale of The Three Billy Goats Gruff reveals the consequences of unchecked hunger and the importance of balance. The troll's insatiable greed not only isolates him but leads to his defeat. This story reminds us that true resilience and mental durability come not from hoarding resources or dominating others but from nurturing meaningful connections, practicing moderation, and cultivating self-awareness.

When we learn to manage our desires with balance and humility, we create space for growth, reflection, and genuine connection. Building a durable mind means recognizing that fulfillment is not found in endless accumulation, but in giving, connecting, and contributing to the lives of others. By focusing on generosity, community, and mutual support, we counter the inner void that drives greed and strengthens our mental resilience. True strength lies in living with purpose and compassion, fostering relationships that nourish us and create a lasting sense of fulfillment.

In the end, our hunger for success, validation, or security does not have to lead us down a path of isolation or selfishness. By addressing the root of our desires, embracing community, and practicing generosity, we cultivate a mind that is resilient, balanced, and deeply connected to others.

For more insights and personal stories related to this chapter, listen to Episode 11 of The Life Sculptors Podcast:

- **Episode Title:** "Living Beyond Comparisons."
- **Listen Here:** https://youtu.be/OUnizfjl_VQ

Durability Lab: Strategies for Managing Hunger and Building Balance

The drive for more—whether it's success, validation, or achievement—can be a powerful motivator, but without balance, it can also lead to emotional depletion and disconnection. A durable mind recognizes the importance of managing internal hunger, ensuring that ambition is fueled by purpose rather than fear. The following exercises will help you assess your personal hunger, establish balance, and cultivate a mindset of fulfillment and generosity.

1. **Identify Your Hunger**

Reflect on areas in your life where you feel an insatiable need for more—whether it's career success, approval from others, material gain, or control over circumstances. Ask yourself:

- Is this desire driven by genuine purpose, or is it rooted in fear or insecurity?

- How is this hunger affecting my well-being and relationships?
  Recognizing the source of your hunger allows you to navigate it with clarity, ensuring that your pursuit aligns with your values rather than being driven by external pressures.

2. **Practice Moderation**

Like the troll in *The Three Billy Goats Gruff*, unchecked desires can lead to harmful consequences—whether emotional burnout, strained relationships, or dissatisfaction despite accomplishments. Developing mindfulness practices, such as journaling or meditation, helps you recognize when your hunger is becoming excessive.

To create a sense of balance:

- Set clear boundaries around your ambitions and commitments.
- Engage in activities that replenish rather than drain you.
- Regularly assess whether your goals contribute to your well-being or merely feed an unquenchable appetite.

For additional support, refer to the *Mindfulness Practices for Recognizing Emotional Depletion worksheet in Appendix C.*

3. **Foster Generosity**

One of the most effective ways to temper an insatiable hunger is to shift from consumption to contribution. Instead of focusing on what you lack, focus on what you can give—whether it's time, knowledge, encouragement, or resources. Practicing generosity not only strengthens connections but also builds emotional resilience, reinforcing that fulfillment comes not just from acquiring, but from sharing.

Ways to foster generosity:

- Volunteer your time to a cause that aligns with your values.
- Share your talents or insights with someone who could benefit from them.
- Engage in small daily acts of kindness that shift your focus from scarcity to abundance.

Reader Exercise: The Hunger Scale

Use this exercise to evaluate and manage the hunger that drives you:

1. **Reflect** – Identify one area in your life where you feel a persistent hunger for more (e.g., career, relationships, financial success, recognition).
2. **Evaluate** – On a scale from 1 to 10, rate how this hunger is impacting your mental and emotional well-being.
3. **Balance** – Write down one action you can take to manage this hunger more effectively (e.g., setting healthy limits, practicing gratitude, prioritizing rest, seeking meaningful connection).

Final Thought

Motivation is essential for growth, but unchecked hunger can cloud our judgment and deplete our emotional reserves. A durable mind recognizes when to strive forward and when to pause, reflect, and realign. By practicing self-awareness, moderation, and generosity, you can maintain balance, ensuring that your ambition is a force for progress rather than a source of exhaustion.

Chapter 10 Durability Reflection Questions

- As you reflect on this chapter, consider how hunger, greed, or desperation may be affecting your own life. Remember, true strength lies not in having more, but in knowing when enough is enough and creating space for connection and growth.
- Are there areas where you feel the need for more, and how might addressing those emotional roots help you build a more durable mind?
- What desires or "hungers" in your life might be driving you toward choices that feel isolating or unbalanced? How can you approach these desires with more self-awareness and moderation?
- In what areas of your life could practicing generosity or building stronger connections with others help counter feelings of inadequacy or the need for control?
- Think about a time when unchecked ambition or desire led to feelings of burnout or emotional depletion. What could practice moderation or fostering meaningful relationships have changed about that experience?

NOTES

DURABILITY LAB MILESTONE #5

Sustaining Motivation and Building Long-Term Endurance

The Durability Lab Milestones are designed to track your growth, ensure accountability, and celebrate your wins. This final milestone is about sustaining motivation, managing your internal hunger, and cultivating a balanced, purpose-driven mindset that keeps you moving forward without burning out.

Motivation Tracker: The Progress Check-In

Use this simple framework to assess your motivation levels and recognize patterns in what fuels or drains your energy:

Marker: Each week, reflect on the following:

- ✓ What inspired me most this week?
- ✓ Where did I feel the most resistance, and how did I push through?
- ✓ What habits or strategies helped me stay motivated and balanced?

The Giving Back Challenge

True motivation is fueled by purpose—not just personal success, but how you impact others. Challenge yourself to engage in acts of generosity that reignite your motivation and reinforce the value of contribution.

Marker: Choose one of the following to complete this week:

- ✓ Mentor or encourage someone who could benefit from your knowledge.
- ✓ Share your progress with a trusted friend or accountability partner.

- ✓ Perform an act of generosity that reminds you of the greater purpose behind your motivation.

Future Self Reflection: Writing a Letter to Yourself

This milestone is about **sustaining momentum beyond this book**. Take a moment to write a letter to your future self, encouraging them to stay committed to the growth you've cultivated.

Marker: Write about:

- ✓ ✔ What you've learned about your motivation and resilience.
- ✓ ✔ The biggest shift you've experienced in how you think and act.
- ✓ ✔ A piece of advice you'd give yourself for staying on track in the months ahead.

Final Thought

A durable mind is not just built in moments of challenge, but in the daily habits that sustain motivation over time. This final milestone is an invitation to continue your journey, staying connected to your purpose, your progress, and your potential. Keep striving, keep growing, and most of all—**keep moving forward.**

EPILOGUE-THE JOURNEY FORWARD

A durable mind is not something we are born with—it is something we build, shape, and strengthen over time. It requires conscious effort, intentional reflection, and a willingness to embrace both struggle and growth. Our imagination plays a pivotal role in this process. Like any tool, it can be an asset that propels us forward or a liability that keeps us stuck. When we actively choose our perspective, we harness imagination as a force for progress. But when we allow circumstances to dictate our outlook, we risk making our imagination a barrier—an internal weapon formed against our own peace and purpose. A durable mind does not passively accept external narratives; instead, it takes accountability for shaping its own story, choosing curiosity over fear and adaptability over stagnation.

In their book *The Breakthrough Manifesto*, authors Kim Christfort and Suzanne Vickberg present that as we get older, we view mess and uncertainty as disruptive, imperfect, uncontrolled, and a threat to the status quo that should be avoided rather than opportunities. A durable mind needs space to get a little messy in order to creatively explore other possibilities. Progress is rarely linear—it is often unpredictable and, at times, messy. When we resist this natural process, we risk becoming stuck in rigid patterns. Limiting our headspace to what is known and controlled, places our focus on the outcome and we miss the benefits of the process. Maybe our definition of what is "right" needs to be reexamined and continuously challenged by our continued growth and which would offer a reframe of mess that is worth considering. What if we reframed our thinking from "making a mess" to "practical experimentation"? Instead of fearing uncertainty, we can embrace it as an opportunity to refine our thinking, explore new approaches, and test-drive or "try on" our perspectives like we would a new car or a new pair of shoes.

My Personal Journey Toward Durability

I had to learn to make room for other ways of thinking and doing so that I could show up in life in a way that was more settled and steadier. From that teary moment at my desk to now, I have experienced both victories and challenges that have developed my ability to be more resilient. Reinventing my career from full-time principal to full-time entrepreneur has been the most difficult and courageous career move I have ever made. Throughout this transition, there were many moments when I felt like things were caving in on me. I often responded like the characters in the children's books I was reading on my podcast.

The conversations I was having with my audience always began as conversations I was having with myself. I questioned my ability to accomplish this work. As I battled my thoughts and sorted through my emotions, it became clearer that progress was being made, even when I felt like turning back. Surrendering to the process and leaning into discomfort taught me the importance of extending grace to myself. I recognized that I was not always listening to my best advice—I needed others, my community. There were moments when I maintained focus and others when I became my biggest distraction. Progress was messy and unpredictable, but I learned that it was worth the investment.

As I practiced Determination, Resilience, Exploration, Adaptability, and Motivation—the five keys to a durable mind—I found myself growing in ways I never expected. Through regular exercise, mindfulness, coaching, journaling, reading, spiritual practices, and meaningful connections, I developed the strength to endure. Developing a durable mind required me to step away from the instinct to use "armor" to protect myself. Vulnerability became my greatest strength. By embracing this, I was able to realized that true durability requires it and that letting go of fear and self-doubt opened the door to deeper resilience, stronger relationships, and a more fulfilling life.

The Five Keys to a Durable Mind in Action

Each of the **5 Keys to Developing a Durable Mind** played a role in my personal journey, and they can serve as guideposts for yours:

- **Determination** *(Chapters 1 & 2)* taught me to push forward even when my confidence wavered. I learned that connection and clarifying my expectations consistently is more powerful than motivation alone.
- **Resilience** *(Chapters 3 & 4)* helped me embrace setbacks as steppingstones, recognizing that obstacles do not signal failure, they refine strength.
- **Exploration** *(Chapters 5 & 6)* encouraged me to remain curious, seek new perspectives, and step beyond my comfort zone.
- **Adaptability** *(Chapters 7 & 8)* reminded me that rigidity limits growth. The more willing I was to pivot and adjust, thc stronger I became.
- **Motivation** *(Chapters 9 & 10)* helped me sustain my journey. I learned that external achievements alone cannot sustain long-term resilience—purpose, service, and connection fuel true motivation.

Each of these five keys helped me move beyond survival mode and into a mindset of continuous growth. And they can do the same for you.

Conclusion

Life will always present unexpected turns, setbacks, and moments of uncertainty. The beauty of a durable mind is that it does not seek to avoid these hardships but instead learns to embrace them, finding strength, wisdom, and purpose in the process. A durable mind sees challenges as opportunities to grow, losses as invitations to reflect, and obstacles as doorways to new paths. This mindset does not ignore reality; it accepts it, navigates it, and learns from it.

The stories within these pages remind us that resilience is deeply connected to the heart. To endure and thrive, we need compassion—for ourselves and others. We need courage to venture beyond the familiar, persistence to keep going, and patience to trust the timing of our journey. We need humility to accept support from others and the wisdom to offer it in return.

In the end, developing a durable mind is about building a foundation that can support us through whatever lies ahead. It is a lifelong practice, one that evolves as we grow and encounter new experiences. May you carry these lessons forward, returning to them as often as needed, allowing them to guide you through each season of life. Remember, resilience is not an innate trait but a skill that is honed through intention, reflection, and action. Each day offers us the chance to build strength, cultivate resilience, and forge a path of purpose.

As you go forward, remember: the mind, like the heart, grows stronger with each test, each lesson, and each step forward. A durable mind is not built in isolation—it is built through connection, understanding, and intentional action. Embrace this journey, trust in your capacity to grow, and keep striving toward the resilience and strength that lies within you. See this book not as a set of strategies, but as an invitation to reflect, to challenge yourself, and to step boldly into the next season of your life with greater confidence, clarity, and courage.

May you carry these lessons with you, returning to them whenever you need guidance. May you continue seeking, growing, and embracing the process. And above all, may you trust in your own capacity to thrive, no matter what challenges arise.

With resilience, gratitude and on purpose,

Dante

APPENDIX

APPENDIX A

Companion Podcast Episodes: Expanding Your Durable Mind

To deepen your journey toward mental resilience, each chapter in this book is paired with a corresponding podcast episode from the *Developing a Durable Mind* series. These episodes provide further insights, personal stories, and practical strategies to reinforce the themes explored in each chapter.

How to Use This Appendix:

- Listen to the podcast episodes as a supplement to each chapter.
- Reflect on the discussions and take notes on insights that resonate with you.
- Use the episodes to revisit key concepts and deepen your understanding of mental durability.

By integrating these resources, you will gain even more tools and perspectives to build resilience and thrive in life's challenges.

Chapter 1: Developing a Durable Mind Through Connection

- Episode Title: *"Finding Peace Through Difficult Relationships"*
- Listen Here: https://youtu.be/B54E-nQmhag

Chapter 2: Managing Expectations – The Foundation of a Durable Mind

- Episode Title: *"What To Do When Things Aren't Going Right."*
- Listen Here: https://youtu.be/P4oI9sjd8YI (part 1) and https://youtu.be/YqskKdRh0KA (part 2)

Chapter 3: Getting Unstuck – Building Mental Flexibility

- Episode Title: *"How To Get Unstuck."*
- Listen Here: https://youtu.be/B8vI5Mixs5A

Chapter 4: Dreams and Determination – Building Strength Through Persistence

- Episode Title: *"Learning to Live Between the Now, Not Yet & Not Possible."*
- Listen Here: https://youtu.be/3Wy3g55AYk4

Chapter 5: Compassion – Hidden Strengths and the Power of Empathy

- Episode Title: *"Don't Be Lame. Be Compassionate."*
- Listen Here: https://youtu.be/l7m-ihCi5fg

Chapter 6: The Quest for Curiosity – Building Mental Flexibility and Growth

- Episode Title: "*Who You? The Quest for Curiosity."*
- Listen Here: https://youtu.be/6KYuM2Hm4dc

Chapter 7: The Power of Patience in Strengthening Your Resilience

- Episode Title: "*Why Waiting Is So Hard."*
- Listen Here: https://youtu.be/5xLQb9IzL38

Chapter 8: Learning from Mistakes – The Path to Building Resilience

- Episode Title: *"Mistakes Happen. Moving Forward Is A Choice."*
- Listen Here: https://youtu.be/xGgVnUwf87o

Chapter 9: The Armor of Appearance and Attitude – Defenses Against Hurt

- Episode Title*: "Enough Is Enough. Stop Isolating. Start Insulating."*

- Listen Here: https://youtu.be/p58oSKpIznM

Chapter 10: Managing Hunger – The Drive for a Durable Mind

- Episode Title: "*Living Beyond Comparisons.*"

- Listen Here: https://youtu.be/OUnizfjl_VQ

APPENDIX B

Expanding Emotional Awareness Through Granularity

Instructions:

- Throughout your week, take time each day to identify an emotion you are experiencing.
- Use the **Emotional Granularity Chart** to find a more specific and nuanced word to describe it.
- Reflect on how that emotion impacted your thoughts and actions.

Worksheet: Emotional Granularity Tracker

Date	Initial Emotion (Broad Category)	More Specific Emotion	Trigger/Event	How Did You Respond?	What Could Help Regulate or Shift the Emotion?
Example	Sadness	Disappointed	Missed a deadline at work	Became self-critical and withdrawn	Self-compassion, reframing mistakes as learning opportunities

Date	Initial Emotion (Broad Category)	More Specific Emotion	Trigger/Event	How Did You Respond?	What Could Help Regulate or Shift the Emotion?

Reflection Questions:

1. What patterns do you notice in your emotional responses?
2. Are certain emotions harder to identify than others?
3. What strategies help you regulate or shift difficult emotions?
4. Are there recurring triggers that influence your emotions?
5. How does naming your emotions more precisely impact your ability to cope with them?

Bonus Activity:

- **Journaling Prompt:** Choose one emotion from your week and write about it in depth. Where did you feel it in your body? What thoughts accompanied it? How did it influence your actions?

- **Mindfulness Practice:** The next time you experience a strong emotion, pause and name it before reacting. Try to replace "I feel bad" with "I feel disheartened because…"

APPENDIX C

Worksheet: Mindfulness Practices for Recognizing Emotional Depletion

Introduction

This worksheet is designed to help you engage in mindfulness practices that foster emotional awareness and resilience. Use these exercises to identify patterns of emotional depletion and disconnection and explore ways to reconnect with yourself.

Part 1: Emotional Awareness Check-In

1. **Body Scan Meditation**

- **Instructions:** Close your eyes and take a few deep breaths. Starting from your toes and moving upward, focus on each part of your body. Note areas of tension, discomfort, or relaxation.
- **Reflcction:** What sensations did you notice in your body? What might these indicate about your emotional state?

Body Part	Sensation Observed	Possible Emotional Link
Toes		
Legs		
Stomach		
Chest		
Shoulders		
Head		

2. **Emotion Naming**

- **Instructions:** Take a moment to pause and ask yourself, "What am I feeling right now?" Use the *Feelings Wheel* or similar tools to name your emotions.
- **Prompt:** Write down three emotions you are experiencing and explore why you might be feeling this way.

Emotion Possible Trigger or Cause Thoughts/Reflections

Part 2: Mindfulness Exercises

3. Five Senses Exercise

- Instructions: Engage with the present moment by observing:
    - 5 things you can see.
    - 4 things you can hear.
    - 3 things you can feel.
    - 2 things you can smell.
    - 1 thing you can taste.

Sense	**Observations**
Sight	
Hearing	
Touch	
Smell	
Taste	

- **Reflection:** How did this exercise make you feel? Did it help ground you in the moment?

4. 4. Gratitude Check-In

- **Instructions:** Write down three things you are grateful for today. Consider both big and small aspects of your life.

Gratitude Item	Why It Matters to You

Part 3: Energy and Reflection

5. **Energy Check-In**

- **Instructions:** Rate your emotional and physical energy on a scale of 1 to 10 at the following times.

Time of Day	**Emotional Energy (1-10)**	**Physical Energy (1-10)**
Morning		
Midday		
Evening		

- **Reflection:** What patterns did you notice? What might be contributing to energy highs or lows?

6. **Self-Compassion Break**

- **Instructions:** When you notice emotional depletion, pause and reflect:

    1. **Acknowledge:** "This is a moment of suffering."
    2. **Normalize:** "Suffering is a part of life."
    3. **Be Kind:** "May I be kind to myself in this moment."

- **Reflection:** How did this practice affect your mood or mindset?

Part 4: Weekly Summary

7. **7. Weekly Reflection**

- What mindfulness practices resonated with you the most?
- What patterns of emotional depletion or connection did you observe?
- What steps will you take next week to build on your progress?

Observations Insights Gained Actions for Next Week

Conclusion

Regular mindfulness practice can help you recognize emotional depletion and reconnect with your inner strength. Use this worksheet consistently to build awareness, foster resilience, and cultivate a more durable mind.

APPENDIX D

Curiosity Map Worksheet

Developing a Durable Mind Through Exploration and Inquiry

Curiosity is a powerful tool for resilience, problem-solving, and personal growth. This worksheet will guide you in using a **Curiosity Map** to explore challenges, uncover opportunities, and develop new strategies for navigating uncertainty.

Step 1: Define Your Challenge or Goal

Write your challenge, problem, or goal in the center of a blank page. Keep it specific and clear.

📌 **Example**: "How can I improve my confidence in public speaking?"

Step 2: Generate Open-Ended Questions

Surround your challenge with open-ended questions that encourage deeper thinking. These questions should help you look at the situation from multiple angles.

Consider questions like:

- What is holding me back?
- Who can I learn from?
- What new approach can I try?
- What am I missing?
- What resources or tools could help?

- How have others navigated similar challenges?
- What strengths do I already have that can help me?

Step 3: Brainstorm Possible Solutions or Next Steps

For each question, jot down at least one possible answer, solution, or action step.

📌 **Example:**

Challenge: "How can I improve my confidence in public speaking?"

Questions	Possible Solutions / Actions
What is holding me back?	Fear of judgment – practice with a supportive group first.
Who can I learn from?	Watch TED Talks and study great speakers' techniques.
What new approach can I try?	Join a local Toastmasters club to practice in a structured setting.
What am I missing?	More preparation and scripting – practice with a mirror or record yourself.

Step 4: Identify Patterns and Choose an Action Step

- Look for recurring themes in your answers.
- Which solutions feel the most actionable?
- Select **one** action step to implement immediately.

📌 **Example:** "I will practice speaking in front of a small group of friends and ask for feedback."

Step 5: Reflect on the Experience

After trying your selected action, take a moment to reflect:

- What worked well?
- What challenges did you face?
- What did you learn about yourself?
- What adjustments can you make moving forward?

Final Thoughts

A Curiosity Map is a tool you can return to whenever you feel stuck or uncertain. By continuously asking questions and exploring possibilities, you cultivate **mental flexibility, adaptability,** and **resilience**—key components of a durable mind.

APPENDIX E-FURTHER READING

1. Barrett, Lisa Feldman. *How Emotions Are Made: The Secret Life of the Brain.* Houghton Mifflin Harcourt, 2017.
2. Bright, Jill Wolf. *A Frog Thing.* Kidwick Books, 2005.
3. Brown, Brené. *Atlas of the Heart: Mapping Meaningful Connection and the Language of Human Experience.* Random House, 2021.
4. Brown, Brené. *Daring Greatly: How the Courage to Be Vulnerable Transforms the Way We Live, Love, Parent, and Lead.* Gotham Books, 2012.
5. Clark, Dan. *Puppies for Sale.* Pelican Publishing, 1997.
6. Clanton, Alex. *Unicorns Are the Worst.* Simon & Schuster Books for Young Readers, 2020.
7. Coligiovanni, Marc. *When Things Don't Go Right, Go Left.* Roaring Brook Press, 2023.
8. Cooks-Campbell, A. (2022, June 2). "When Tough Isn't Enough, Build Mental Strength. Here's How." Better Up. Retrieved from https://www.betterup.com/blog/mental-strength.
9. Couto, D. (2003). "I Was Greedy, Too." *Harvard Business Review.* Retrieved from www.hbr.org.
10. Denise, Christopher. *Knight Owl.* Little, Brown Books for Young Readers, 2022.
11. Festinger, L. (1957). *A Theory of Cognitive Dissonance.* Stanford University Press.

12. Frankl, Viktor E. *Man's Search for Meaning.* Beacon Press, 2006.

13. Gilbert, P., & Choden. (2014). *Mindful compassion: Using the power of mindfulness and compassion to transform our lives*. New Harbinger Publications.

14. Goodrich, Carter. *Nobody Hugs a Cactus.* Simon & Schuster Books for Young Readers, 2019.

15. Ivtzan, I., Young, T., Martman, J., & Jeffrey, A. (2021). *Mindfulness-based positive psychology interventions and their role in fostering psychological resilience*. BMC Psychology. Retrieved from https://bmcpsychology.biomedcentral.com/articles/10.1186/s40359-021-00618-2

16. Jeffers, Oliver. *Stuck.* Philomel Books, 2011.

17. Jannazzo, E. S. (2019, June 12). "What Is Maturity? Authentically Creating a Refuge in an Age of Anxiety." *Psychology Today.* Retrieved from https://www.psychologytoday.com/us/blog/the-full-spectrum/201906/what-is-maturity.

18. Kalb, Bess. *Buffalo Fluffalo.* Random House Studio, 2024.

19. Kashdan, T. B. (2009). Curious: Discover the Missing Ingredient to a Fulfilling Life. HarperCollins.

20. Santat, Dan. *After the Fall: How Humpty Dumpty Got Back Up Again.* Roaring Brook Press, 2017.

21. Vickberg, K. C. (2024). *The Breakthrough Manifesto: 10 Principles to Spark Transformative Innovation.* John Wiley & Sons, Inc.

22. Yamada, Kobi. *What Do You Do with an Idea?* Compendium Inc., 2014.

DEVELOPING A DURABLE MIND

Developing a Durable Mind explores resilience, mental flexibility, and thriving through challenges. Drawing from children's stories and reflections, it offers insights on persistence, curiosity, connection, self-compassion, and vulnerability. The book shows how setbacks can lead to growth and emphasizes the importance of patience and community. It includes practical strategies, reflective questions, and examples to help readers build a resilient mindset. Aimed at leaders, professionals, and anyone seeking personal growth, it equips readers to face adversity with strength and hope, embracing life's complexities and fostering a durable mind in a changing world.

"Dante's Developing a Durable Mind is a powerful homage to the process—one he has lived, refined, and now generously shares. With a career built on resilience, he curates a book that is both profound and playful, delivering empowerment, education, and enlightenment through the simplicity of a children's book. It's a reminder that we are all, at our core, just big kids—deserving of the tools to develop a durable mind in an increasingly fragile world."

MARY HEMPHILL, PhD
CEO & Founder of Limitless

"If you are a follower of Brene Brown's work, you will love Dante Poole's "Developing a Durable Mind!" Dante insightfully weaves together the wisdom of children's literature, insights from mindfulness scholarship, and skills building exercises honed from his 30+ years of experience within the educational profession. Each chapter creatively begins with a core insight gleaned from an illustrated children's book and builds on that insight to develop a set of Durability Lab skill-building exercises. Readers who faithfully complete the exercises will undoubtedly cultivate a strong and adaptable Durable Mind. This book is essential reading for everyone working in the human services sector."

MARYLOU RAMSEY
EdD, Professor Emeritus, Department of Counselor Education, The College of New Jersey

"Developing a Durable Mind is distinct in its presentation in that it is both exhaustive and comprehensive; simple in presentation, yet extensive in application. Dante Poole has reimagined how we can better think about ourselves, others, and life (in general)by producing a blueprint – a roadmap – for the journey of transformation. This work is not about changing one's mind, but transforming the foundational basis of thought itself; a healthier me, a healthier you, for a healthier us."

REV. DR. MIKE BASS
Dean Solid Rock School of Theology; the Global Methodist Church

ABOUT THE AUTHOR

Dante Poole is an accomplished leadership and relationship coach, keynote speaker, trainer, and former principal with over 30 years of experience in education, coaching, and personal development. As the founder of Life Sculptors LLC, he is dedicated to empowering individuals and organizations to develop resilience, emotional intelligence, and meaningful connections. A TEDx speaker and award-winning educator, Dante's work blends practical strategies with deep insights to foster personal and professional growth. His expertise in leadership, coaching, and emotional resilience has made him a sought-after speaker and consultant. In Developing a Durable Mind: A Guide to Cultivating Strength and Adaptability, he shares his passion for helping others build mental resilience, navigate challenges, and thrive in an ever-changing world.

Made in the USA
Columbia, SC
24 March 2025